PUB WALKS ON DARTMOOR

Laurence Main

Published by Sigma Leisure – an imprint of
Sigma Press, 1 South Oak Lane, Wilmslow, Cheshire SK9 6AR, England.

British Library Cataloguing in Publication Data
A CIP record for this book is available from the British Library.

ISBN: 1-85058-358-7

Typesetting and Design by: Sigma Press, Wilmslow, Cheshire.

Maps by: Morag Perrott

Text photographs: Laurence Main

Cover photograph: The Old Inn, Widecombe-in-the-Moor (photograph by Hamilton-Fisher)

Printed by: Manchester Free Press

General Disclaimer

Whilst every effort has been made to ensure that the information given in this book is correct, neither the publisher nor the author accept any responsibility for any inaccuracy.

Preface

Southern England is not supposed to have a wilderness that reaches to over 2000 feet above sea level. Yet this is what we have in Dartmoor, whose highest point is the 2039 feet of High Willhays. So valuable is the untamed and breathtaking scenery of Dartmoor that it has become a National Park. The visionaries who designated it as such did so with the intention of encouraging public access for open-air recreation, as well as sustaining the local way of life.

The only way to experience Dartmoor properly is on foot. However fine the view from the B3212 or the other roads that traverse Dartmoor, it cannot compare with the joy of feeling the wind in your hair. Cars cannot reach the wildest and most beautiful parts of the moor. Because such a high wilderness is such a novelty to people in the South of England, there is a tendency for them to exaggerate the dangers of Dartmoor. People are supposed to have disappeared without trace in its bogs, but researching these walks in the wettest summer for some years revealed only some areas of waterlogged ground. By its nature, moorland is fairly featureless, while mist can descend at any time (sometimes there is what can only be described as a permanent 'mizzle'). You may get lost, cold and wet, so the Ordnance Survey maps must be acquired and used. A good compass is also highly recommended, for use with the maps. If you do get lost, retrace your steps to your last known position.

The Ordnance Survey has made the business of acquiring maps easier by producing an excellent Outdoor Leisure map (No. 28) which covers very nearly all of the National Park. Once obtained, it would be a good idea to make it waterproof, perhaps by spraying it with Texnik. A few other maps are also needed. It would be a pity to leave out the eastern and western edges of Dartmoor just because they are excluded from the Outdoor Leisure map. There are some good pubs there and some fine walking territory with such attractions as Brent Tor and Dunsford. The details of the relevant Ordnance Survey Pathfinder maps for these areas are given with the information on maps for individual walks. Where there is also a Pathfinder map covering the whole route of a walk which is on the Outdoor Leisure map, this is mentioned as well. Pathfinders are a more convenient size than the Outdoor Leisure map.

Walking boots should be your best friend on Dartmoor. Overtrousers may be welcomed by some, but if you wear shorts you'll find that bare legs dry easily. A good anorak is essential, as is a lightweight rucksack for carrying it. Take spare clothing and some food and drink as well – and it's always a good idea to have an emergency first-aid kit of patches, antiseptic cream and pain-relieving tablets. A torch and batteries should also be carried, but avoid getting lost in the dark by allowing plenty of time for each walk to be completed in daylight. Two miles per hour is what most people manage.

There is one danger that must be avoided, although none of these walks is affected – with Walk 2 (Nine Stones) coming closest to the action, and numbers 4 (South Zeal) and 10 (Widgery Cross) not far behind. Military training with live firing takes place on Dartmoor. Non-firing periods are specified so that the public can know when to enjoy access to the ranges. Pick up a special leaflet on this subject at a Dartmoor National Park Visitor Centre. Expect to be able to walk freely at weekends throughout the year, over Easter, during the summer and over Christmas. There is a telephone answering service to keep you informed about firing programmes, using the following numbers: Torquay (0803) 294592, Exeter (0392) 70164, Plymouth (0752) 701924 and Okehampton (0837) 52939.

Walking is the 'greenest' form of tourism, so be consistent by caring for the environment of Dartmoor and refusing to drive a car there. Access to the starts of all these walks can be achieved by bus, as detailed in the information on access for each individual walk. Devon County Council produce a free timetable for the bus services on Dartmoor. Send an A5 SAE (100g rate) for a copy to Devon County Council, Luscombe House, Topsham Road, Exeter, EX2 4QW. There is also a County Council Enquiry Line (8.30 am to 5 pm Mondays to Fridays) on 0392 382800.

The National Park Authority operates information centres at Princetown (open all year, telephone 082289 414), Postbridge (seasonal), Steps Bridge (seasonal), Newbridge (seasonal), Parke Barn (seasonal), Tavistock (seasonal) and Okehampton (seasonal), while South Hams District Council's Tourist Information Centre at Ivybridge is open all year.

Laurence Main

Contents

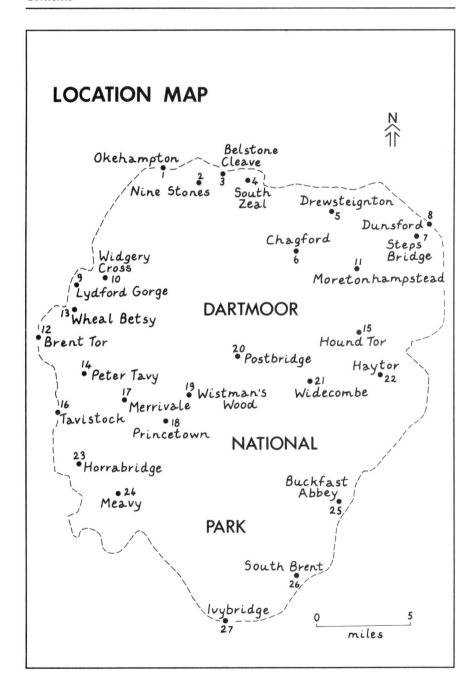

Introduction

Dartmoor National Park comprises 365 square miles of high, rolling upland. The highest ground, reaching to over 2000 feet, is in the North Moor, while the River Dart divides the South Moor from the East Moor. The most spectacular scenery is on the East Moor, with the North and South Moors more monotonously peat-covered plateaux. The East Moor has more tors or jagged outcrops, while rivers run through scenic 'cleaves' or gorges.

The wet climate is tempered by the warmer temperatures at this latitude, in contrast to the moorland of northern Britain. Do not be surprised by gales. The prevailing wind is south westerly and the weather forecast seems always to be of rain spreading from the west ... The western side of Dartmoor averages over 100 inches of rain in a year, reducing to 60 inches as you go eastwards. Remember too that the villages, pubs and campsites are on a plateau, not down in a valley. This makes for cold nights, especially if you are camping. Snow can be expected in winter. On the other hand there are rumours of hot, sunny, summer days!

The plantlife reflects Dartmoor's mixture of harsh northern moorland in a softer southern setting. Upland birds make this their most southern breeding habitat. Mammals also find homes in the broad-leaved woods that have survived in the steep valleys on the upland fringe. Dartmooor has the distinction of being the only national park with a bigger area covered by broad-leaved trees rather than exotic conifers.

About 30,000 people actually live within the boundary of the national park, with agriculture employing about one in eight of the 10,000 or so who are in work. Nearly all of Dartmoor (87%) is farmed, however, with nearly half of the area (40%) being registered as common land. There is a tradition for the land to be used on a seasonal basis by people in other parts of Devon.

People have left their mark on Dartmoor's landscape, from ancient and enigmatic standing stones through to tin mines. In this respect, there is a Celtic (to be precise, a pre-Celtic) aura about the place which gives it more the feel of Cornwall. Devon and Cornwall used to form a single Celtic kingdom (Dumnonia) but the Saxons gained control of the more fertile ground of Devon fairly soon after 700, if not before.

Dartmoor was once (400 million years ago) on the floor of a sea. The slates now found here were originally sediments deposited in the sea by rivers which flowed from mountains to the north. These sedimentary rocks were folded by intense pressure to form the Cornubian Mountains about 290 million years ago (Late Carboniferous period). Magma welled up from beneath these folds and cooled to form granite. The scene changed radically during the Cretaceous period, some 175 to 145 million years ago, by which time the Cornubian Mountains had been eroded away and Dartmoor was under a shallow sea, resulting in the deposition of a layer of chalk. This had been eroded away by the Tertiary period, 75 million years ago when rivers and general weathering also affected the granite.

The characteristic tors of Dartmoor were domed granite outcrops which rose about the evergreen forests of the Tertiary period. These were attached by chemical and mechanical weathering. When Arctic conditions prevailed in the Pleistocene Ice Age (600,000 to 10,000 years ago), the constant freezing and thawing of water along the joints broke up the exposed granite. The local word 'clitter' describes the blocks that have fallen around the feet of the tors. After the Ice Age, temperate forest formed of hazel, oak, birch and elm spread over Dartmoor. As people cleared this forest for grazing, the uncovered soil now deprived of humus was leached away. Thus was the moorland created.

There were no national park boundaries in prehistory, of course. The people who lived on Dartmoor may well have wintered in the lowlands and driven their animals up to Dartmoor on a seasonal basis. The early hunters probably migrated in pursuit of their prey. The first evidence of forest clearance is for around 3500 BC, in the New Stone Age. Permanent settlements may have existed on Dartmoor by then although transhumance was probably still practised, or groups would clear a small area, exploit its soil and move on.

Metal-workers arrived around 2500 BC. They erected the standing stones and other enigmatic monuments. Nowhere has such an intense collection of stone rows as Dartmoor. The stone circles are also impressive. The most remarkable relics may be the Dartmoor Reeves. Possibly, prehistoric land divisions (linked to transhumance from the lowlands and reflected in later parish boundaries?) these linear features are reviewed in Andrew Fleming's excellent book *The Dartmoor Reaves*. Dating from about 1700 BC, these long straight walls are contemporary with the prehistoric houses marked by their foundation stones and known as hut circles. Their exploitation of the moor left it sparsely populated from about 1000 to 500 BC. Even this seems to have disappeared in the Iron Age, although a few hillforts are found about the wooded gorges around the fringe of Dartmoor, as with Cranbrook near the River Teign.

The transition from Bronze Age to Iron Age seems to have deeply affected the prosperity of this tin and copper producing area. No Roman remains have been found on Dartmoor. There were Celts here when the Saxons invaded, however, if only in retreat from their lost lowland territories. Lydford, on the western edge of Dartmoor has a Celtic feel to it and a church dedicated to St Petroc (a Celt), who has another church dedicated to him at Harford (north of Ivybridge).

The eastern part of Celtic Dumnonia became Saxon Devon soon after Ine and Nunna of Wessex defeated the gallant Geraint in 710. The high moorland would have been the place for Celtic remnants to survive, while the Saxons are known to have cleared the forests in the valleys. There were settlements on the high moor, as with the medieval hamlet of Houndtor, near Manaton, the final phase of which dates from about 1300. Pollen analysis shows that oats and rye were grown here, above the 100 foot contour. Three of the buildings there have kilns and areas for drying corn. There were also enclosures for animals or kitchen gardens. A deterioration in the climate probably caused the inhabitants to desert this site. An alternative explanation might be the Black Death which arrived in England in 1348. The upland settlement was isolated but plague would have spread very quickly through its tight cluster of dwellings.

Dartmoor was established as a Royal Forest, probably in the 11th century. This meant it was a royal hunting ground rather than covered by trees. The pressure to bring more land under cultivation may have caused the area to be removed from Forest Law in 1239. Still known as the Forest of Dartmoor, the central zone was now a chase (a place for nobles to go hunting) and was granted by the Crown to the Earl of Cornwall. The open moor was also becoming important for grazing sheep to meet the demands of the wool trade. Agriculture's hold was a tenuous one, however, and both arable and pastoral farming were soon discontinued.

Dartmoor's prosperity was linked once more to tin from the 16th century. The tinners had been around in Saxon times, while Lydford Castle's sinister walls were built in 1195 as a prison for offenders against the stannary laws as well as those of the Forest. Earlier, the Danes had been bribed to leave the Saxons in peace with coins minted at Lydford from local metal. Market towns grew up at Okehampton, Tavistock, Chagford, Bovey Tracey, Moretonhampstead, Buckfastleigh, South Brent, Ashburton and Lydford. South Zeal was created as a borough around 1264 but failed to grow. By 1328, the important stannary towns, where tin was collected, taxed and coined, were Chagford, Ashburton, Tavistock and Plympton. The important fulling mills for the woollen industry were also situated in the market towns. Water power was a key factor, as with the Rivers Mardle and Dart at Buckfastleigh. Here, too, stood one of Dartmoor's great abbeys (the only one if you rigidly exclude Tavistock for being just outside the national park boundary). Their wealth came from Dartmoor's sheep. The monks may have erected clapper bridges, as at Postbridge, along the prehistoric trackways. The so-called Abbots Way crosses the moor to link the abbeys at Tavistock and Buckfast. An easier route just to the north of it is lined with crosses and called the Maltern Way, while it is interesting that the Lich Way (for the spirits of the dead?) would link the 35 Ancient Tenements that lie in a peculiarly sheltered position within the Forest along the valleys of the West and East Dart rivers, held by custom for time out of mind and enclosed by the ancient reave builders, with Lydford, with its Celtic church, Devil's Cauldron and waterfall whose name and legend links it to the Goddess - all this beside the isolated St Michael's Church at Brent Tor and the famous dragon line of spiritual energy.

Most Dartmoor valleys betray remains of tin streaming, where the early tinners extracted the valuable ore from alluvial beds. Holes in the ground mark ancient furnaces for melting the tin. Water-powered tin mills were in place by the end of the 13th century. Leats, or artificial water courses, fed them with water. This practice gave way to lode-working. Lodes of tin still in place in the parent rock were followed down to as much as 100 feet, forming deep gullies. This change in technique brought Dartmoor's tin production to a peak in the 16th century, with 280 tons of tin mined in 1521. The tinners were known as 'The Old Men of the Moor'.

Tin-mining gave natural links with Cornwall and there was an influx of Cornish miners during the boom years of the 19th century. They brought Methodist chapels as well as their expertise. Shaft mines were dug to follow lodes underground. Large wheels known as engine wheels operated the machinery which pumped the mines and raised the ore.

The distinctive farmhouse of Dartmoor was the longhouse, providing shelter for humans and animals under one roof. The poor communications meant that packhorses, rather than horse and cart, were the standard means of transport on the moor. 'Improvers' built turnpike roads around 1800, but schemes to make Dartmoor fertile only resulted in the construction of its prison.

Rather than change Dartmoor's forbidding wilderness, there has grown a movement to safeguard and respect it. The Dartmoor Preservation Association was founded as long ago as 1883. This was interested in the antiquities as well as the rights of way and commons. National park designation came in 1951. The Dartmoor ponies have declined in numbers, however. No longer needed as packhorses and having been bred with the smaller Shetlands to provide pit ponies during the early years of the 20th century, many are now sold to the meat trade. There are no government subsidies for farmers to keep them as opposed to cattle or sheep.

Dartmoor's surviving oak woodland, clothing the steep-sided valleys, provided charcoal and tanning bark for tanyards at Okehampton, Moretonhampstead, Horrabridge, Tavistock and Sticklepath. Again, water was the crucial source of power. Nowadays the towns of South Devon demand water from moorland reservoirs. Cities also demand stone and Dartmoor granite is still quarried on a commercial scale. The remarkable granite tramway on Haytor bears witness to the feats of the early 19th century, when the British Museum was built of Dartmoor granite. China clay is also dug from Dartmoor.

Tourism is Dartmoor's modern industry, pioneered by men such as William Crossing, whose _Guide_ first appeared in 1909. Whereas the new

railways brought visitors in the 19th century and early 20th century, the modern roads and cars allow people to live in Dartmoor and commute to work in cities like Plymouth and Exeter. Housing developments which do not help the locals are now threatening Dartmoor. The national Park Authority encourages tourists to come by bus, promoting weekend and summer holiday rides from the cities (such as the scenic no 82 route between Plymouth and Exeter by way of Princetown, Two Bridges, Postbridge, Moretonhampstead and Steps Bridge).

Take a bus to the start of the walks!

Rare upland birds, including dunlin and golden plover, make Dartmoor one of their most southern outposts, while birds like the woodlark are found at the northern limit of their territory. This reflects the status of Dartmoor as a large area of wild upland in the very south of Britain. The sub-arctic mingles with the Mediterranean. Dartmoor's ecosystem is rich and varied, comprising open moorland, broad-leaved woodland, conifer plantations, enclosed farmland, rivers and riverbanks. The boggy higher slopes form a peat 'sponge' that is the home of bog-cotton, deer-grass, rushes, sedges and bog mosses. Heather, whortleberry, tormentil and milkwort live on the drier parts. They may conceal adders. The Buzzard is Dartmoor's largest bird of prey.

Summer brings the pied flycatcher, wood warbler and redstart to the broad-leaved valley woods. Some enormous badger setts shielded by the trees may be centuries old. The otter may still be sighted on Dartmoor's rivers, although walkers are more likely to spot mink, descended from those that escaped from a fur farm near Moretonhampstead in the 1950s. Dartmoor's plant and animal life makes for fascinating study.

Real Ale

Global trade has resulted in the strange concept of English people drinking tea from Sri Lanka and coffee from Brazil. Apart from the fact that valuable food-growing land in such poor countries is wasted on growing cash-crops of dubious economic benefit (with most of the cash not going to local people), this has separated us from our history and traditions. England is rich in malting barley and the national drink for thousands of years was ale. Only the brave or those fortunate enough to live near a spring drank water. Ale was safer, having been boiled and containing preservatives.

Ale in the middle ages was thick, sticky and sweet. Exotic spices may have been involved, but hops weren't introduced until around 1400. They added bitterness and flavour and had preservative qualities, but took a long time to catch on in England, after being introduced from Flanders. Henry VIII thought hopped beer was only fit to be drunk by Dutchmen and forbade his brewers to add hops. Nearly all ales contained hops after his reign, however.

Each of the pubs featured in this book serves real ale on draught. This means that the beers are still fermenting when they leave the brewery. This is known as secondary fermentation because it supplements the primary fermentation which took place in the brewers' large brewing vessels. The process continues at a slow pace as the barrels are racked in the pub cellar. Carbon dioxide is produced and escapes through a spile hole. The thirsty walker may receive gravity drawn beer, direct from the barrel, or beer from a hand pump or electric pump attached to the bar. Real ale is free of the carbon dioxide or nitrogen used to force pasteurised (i.e. where the fermentation has been killed off) varieties under pressure out of their kegs. These gassy beers are the ones that need the glossy adverts. They are shunned by lovers of traditional ales.

Many landlords take a different view, however. Traditional real ale is less easy to keep. Great care has to be taken regarding temperature and cleanliness. The draught beer has a very short 'shelf-life' and it takes skill, acquired from both training and experience, to serve a good pint of real ale.

Opening Hours

Under recent legislation pubs in England can now open for a maximum of 12 hours each day on Mondays to Saturdays (being 11 am to 11 pm) and for six and a half hours on Sundays (being noon to 3 pm and 7 pm to 10.30 pm) unless extensions have been granted by local licensing magistrates. Additionally, a growing number of pubs stay open during Sunday afternoons to serve meals, with which alcohol may then be consumed on the premises.

Most country pubs do not find it in their interest to take full advantage of these 'relaxed' hours and tend to stick to the 'traditional' hours of noon to 3 pm and 6 pm to 11 pm or 7 pm to 11 pm. Check each pub individually.

The Walks

Each walk in this book follows rights of way to which you, as a member of the public, have unrestricted access. These are public footpaths, bridleways and by-ways as well as lanes and roads. When surveyed, all these routes were free of obstructions. If you do find any problems, send full details (including grid references) to: The Dartmoor National Park Authority, Parke, Haytor Road, Bovey Tracey, Devon, TQ13 9JQ - Tel 0626 832093; The Dartmoor Preservation Association Secretary, Crossings Cottage, Dousland, Yelverton, Plymouth, Devon; The County Surveyor, Devon County Council, Lucombe House, Topsham Road, Exeter, EX2 4QW - tel 0392 382070; The Devon Area Secretary of the Ramblers' Association (currently Mrs E Linfoot, 14 Blaydon Cottages, Blackborough, Cullompton, Devon, EX15 2HJ, tel 08846 435) and The Ramblers' Association at 1/5 Wandsworth Road, London SW8 2XX, Tel 071 582 6878.

The walks are numbered in sequence (almost) from north to south and are spread all over Dartmoor. Make use of the Ordnance Survey maps detailed for each walk. These are beautiful keys to Dartmoor and anybody walking here should become familiar with them.

The walks average about five miles in length. Several of them link with other walks in this book to allow longer routes to the done in a day, if desired. Other walks can be linked with the aid of public transport

The following walks can be directly linked together:

❑ Walks 2 (Nine Stones) and 3 (Belstone Cleave) together give an eight mile route.

❑ Walks 7 (Steps Bridge) and 8 (Dunsford) connect to make a five mile ramble.

❑ Walks 9 (Lydford Gorge), 13 (Wheal Betsy) and 12 (Brent Tor) can be linked in a chain (in that order) to form a long walk of 16 miles.

All walks should be within the capabilities of anyone of average fitness. Allow about one hour for every two miles, which should enable short breaks to be made. Do not be surprised by the strenuous nature of some routes, which can reach 1800 feet above sea level (although you do not start from sea level, of course). Do remember that even on Dartmoor the physical landscape can change. Keep to the path and treat it as a privilege to walk across the land.

The Country Code

❑ Guard against all risk of fire.

❑ Fasten all gates.

❑ Keep dogs under proper control.

❑ Avoid damaging fences, hedges and walls.

❑ Keep to paths across farmland.

❑ Leave no litter.

❑ Safeguard water supplies.

❑ Protect wildlife, wild plants and trees.

❑ Go carefully on country roads.

❑ Respect the life of the countryside.

1. Okehampton

Route: Okehampton – Fatherford – Lower Halstock – Lovers' Meet Bridge – Okehampton Castle – Okehampton

Distance: 5 miles

Map: O.S. Outdoor Leisure 28, Dartmoor

Start: The Plume of Feathers, Okehampton (Grid Reference SX 588952)

Access: Passenger trains no longer serve Okehampton, which is on the A30 road between Exeter and Launceston. There are several buses converging on the town, including nos 51, 227, 628 and 629 from Exeter, nos 86 and 118 (on certain days) from Plymouth, plus the no 187 from Gunnislake, connecting with the train along the Tamar Valley Line from Plymouth on Sundays, no 86 from Ilfracombe, no 118 from Tavistock, no 227 from Launceston, no 629 from Bude and no 860 from Moretonhampstead.

The Plume of Feathers (0837 52815)

Prince Charles, Prince Andrew and Prince Edward have all supped here – so why not sample the hospitality? This old coaching inn offers real ale, food and bed and breakfast accommodation. Bar opening hours are 11 am to 3 pm and 6.30 pm to 11 pm from Mondays to Wednesdays, 11 am to 11 pm from Thursdays to Saturdays and noon to 3 pm, then 7 pm to 10.30 pm on Sundays.

Okehampton

Okehampton's strategic position on the way from Exeter to Cornwall brought it to a Norman castle and 20th century traffic jams. Of course, the powers that be responded to the latter by withdrawing passenger services on the railway, which was closed altogether west of Okehampton, then building a spanking new by-pass to encourage even more people to drive cars along the A30. It is a pity to by-pass this place, with

The museum and Tourist Information Centre, Okehampton

its interesting Museum of Dartmoor Life. St James' Chapel dominated Fore Street, off which is an authentic Victorian shopping arcade. The romantic ruins of the castle are said to be haunted by the ghost of the evil ·Lady Howard, who is said to have murdered four husbands. The biggest castle in Devon, it was built by the Normans to impose their rule in this area soon after the Battle of Hastings. It passed from the Fitzgilbert family to the de Courtenay family in 1172 but was dismantled after the last member of the family to own it was beheaded in 1538. In the care of English Heritage, it is open daily between 10 am and 6 pm from April to October, from Tuesdays to Sundays between 10 am and 4 pm during the winter months and closed over Christmas and on New Year's Day.

The Walk

1. Go left and turn left up George Street. Continue along Mill Road to pass Simmons Park on your right, cross the East Okement River and reach the Town Mill. Climb the steps here and take the track for Ball Hill.

2. Continue through kissing-gates, across two fields and through woodland. Emerge through a gate.

3. Turn right onto a lane, take a gate and go under the stone railway viaduct at Fatherford. Cross a footbridge over the river, continue

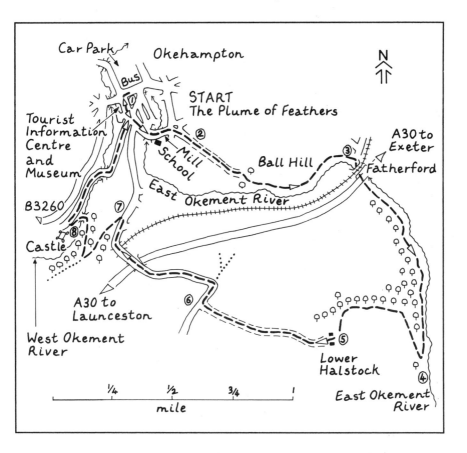

under the A30 road and take the signposted path through the woodland above the East Okement River, on your left. Reach a signposted path junction.

4. Turn sharply right and emerge from the wood at a gate. Go ahead through bracken around a slope to pass a cottage on your left and reach a gate.

5. Bear right to the farmyard at Lowser Halstock and continue along the farm's drive to a road.

6. Go right to follow this road around a bend on your left and over road and rail bridges.

7. Turn left through a kissing-gate to take the signposted path for Okehampton Castle. Turn sharply right to cross the West Okement River to Lovers' Meet bridge. Go left to Okehampton Castle.

8. Bear right along Castle Lane, which becomes Castle Road after crossing the river by Castleford Bridge. Go left when you return to George Street and turn right at Fore Street to return to the Plume of Feathers, on your right.

The Plume of Feathers

2. Nine Stones

Route: Belstone – Higher Tor – Nine Stones – Belstone

Distance: $3^1/_2$ miles

Maps: O.S. Outdoor Leisure 28 Dartmoor, O.S. Pathfinder 1313 Belstone

Start: The Tors Inn (Grid Reference SX 620936)

Access: Belstone is a minor road between Okehampton and Sticklepath. There is a bus (no 860) from Moretonhampstead and Okehampton on Tuesdays, Wednesdays, Fridays and Saturdays. Sticklepath has a better bus service, so why not combine this route with Walk 3 to form a circuit of eight miles?

The Tors Inn (0837 840689)

The Old Inn stood across the road until it was destroyed by a fire in 1896. This is its replacement, adjacent to the graveyard of St Mary's Church. Real ale, food and accommodation are available. Bar opening hours are 11 am to 2.30 pm and 6.30 pm to 11 pm on weekdays, noon to 3 pm and 7 pm to 10.30 pm on Sundays.

N.B. This walk goes near, but not on, Ministry of Defence ranges. To check that firing is not in progress, telephone Plymouth (0752) 701824 or Okehampton (0837) 52939. Notices are also displayed in National Park Information Centres. Firing is not allowed, at present, on every Saturday, Sunday, Monday and Public Holiday, plus during the week beginning and including the Wednesday before Easter, during the months of April, May, July, August and the first 15 days of September, during the week beginning and including the first Sunday in November and between 20th December and 3rd January inclusive.

The Tors

Belstone Common

The tumbledown wall crossing the ridge of Belstone Tor was an attempt to steal part of the common land. Irishmen were employed to erect it, so it is called Irishman's Wall. The local people soon asserted their rights and pushed it down, however. A more mystical set of stones are the Nine Stones. This stone circle has considerably more than none stones and the Michael current that coils around the Dragon Line (of *The Sun and The Serpent* by Hamish Miller and Paul Broadhurst) goes through it on its way between Brent Tor and Crediton. Nine stones or Nine Maidens is a common name for stone monuments (whatever the number of stones). When dowsed, only nine of the stones are found to have energy lines connecting them to the centre within the circle. It also shares a common legend, that Sabbath-breakers were turned to stone for enjoying themselves on a Sunday. Belstone also suggests a link with Bel, the Celtic Sun-God, Belenos the brilliant, or Baal. Bonfires would have been lit on this tor on 1st November, 1st February, 1st May and 1st August (Samhain, Imbolc, Beltane and Lugnasadh).

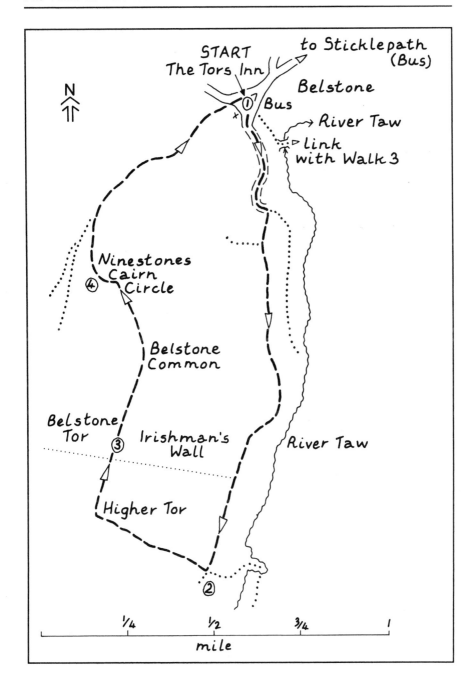

The Walk

1. Walk south of Belstone to pass the church on your right and keep above the River Taw on your left. Follow the hard track until it branches down to a ford in the river at a horseshoe bend.

2. Leave the hard track above the ford but go in the opposite direction to climb Higher Tor. Turn right at the top to follow the ridge to pass through the Irishman's Wall at the summit of the Belstone Tor.

3. Go ahead along Belstone Common and bear left to descend to the Nine Stones (actually this circle has at least 12 stones).

4. Walk north along a track back into Belstone and the Tors Inn.

3. Belstone Cleave

Route: Sticklepath – Belstone – Cleave – Belstone – Belstone Cleave -Skaigh Wood – Sticklepath

Distance: 4$\frac{1}{2}$ miles

Maps: O.S. Outdoor Leisure 28, O.S. Pathfinder 1313 (Belstone and Cheriton Bishop)

Start: The Devonshire Inn, Sticklepath (Grid Reference SX 641 941)

Access: Sticklepath is on the B3260 four miles east of Okehampton. Buses nos 51 and 629 provide a daily service from Okehampton and Exeter.

The Devonshire Inn (0837 840626)

This is a village inn in the original tradition with a linoleum floor 'specially for the walkers'. Real ale and food are served, while 'Lady Gray' walks through the walls! Opening hours are 11 am to 3 pm and 5.30 pm to 11 pm from Mondays to Thursdays, 11 am to 11 pm on Fridays and Saturdays, noon to 3 pm and 7 pm to 10.30 pm on Sundays.

Belstone Cleave

This spectacular walk in the rock-strewn valley of the fast-flowing River Taw is the location for a scene in Henry Williamson's classic story *Tarka the Otter*. Tarka disputed over a rabbit with Swagdagger the stoat, thus putting this path on the Tarka Trail (a walking route of some 180 miles) as well as on the Two Museums Walk (from the Museum of Dartmoor Life in Okehampton to the Museum of Water Power in Finch Foundry, Sticklepath – open 10 am – 5 pm on weekdays, from March to November plus summer Sundays). The local Quakers entertained John Wesley in the village in the 18th century. Tom Pearce's grey mare (of Widecombe Fair fame) was also stabled here.

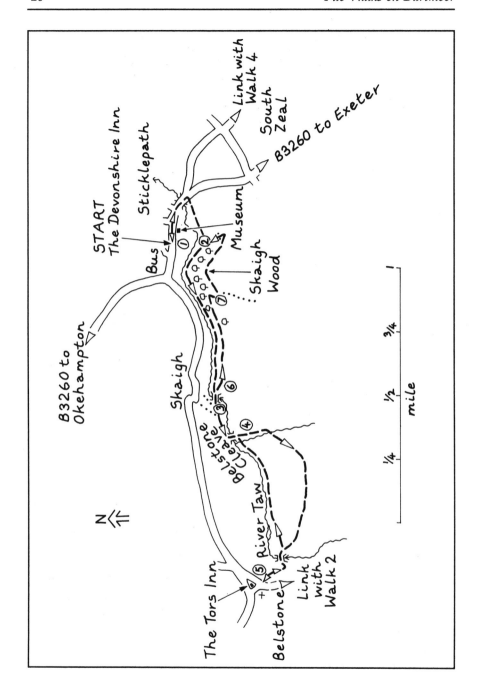

The Walk

1. Go right and soon pass the Museum of Waterpower (Finch Foundry) on your right. Cross the bridge over the River Taw to approach a fork in the road. This won't bother you as you turn right just before the fork to walk with the river on your right. This is signposted as the public bridleway to the Moor and to Skaigh Wood. Follow the firm, hedged, path and ignore two footbridges on your right.

2. Go ahead through a gate and fork right to follow the valley path through Skaigh Wood with the River Taw on your right. Eventually reach a footbridge and go right across it.

3. Follow the path to a junction and turn left to walk with the river on your left in Belstone Cleave. Bear left at a fork to descend to and cross another footbridge.

4. Bear right along the signposted path to the moors and Cawsand. The path climbs gradually then up beside a stream to where it is easy to cross, on your right. Climb above the bracken and keep above the valley on your right. As the river bends, descend to reach a foot-bridge across it near the bend. Continue along a track up to the village of Belstone, where this route may be linked with Walk 2 at the Tors Inn.

5. To complete this walk, retrace your steps down to the footbridge, cross it, turn left but do not take a gate ahead. Bear right with a wall surmounted by a fence on your left. Soon bear left at a fork, to leave your outward route and follow a path running parallel to the river below. Bear left to continue beside the river on your left until a footbridge. Cross this to retrace your steps, but going downstream, to a signpost which reminds you to turn right for the next footbridge, which is crossed again.

6. Bear left along the higher path which runs parallel to the river below. Cross a stile in a fence ahead and turn right to climb a steep zigzag path, keeping near the fence on your right. Reach a signpost beside a gate, on your right.

7. Turn left along the track which keeps just within the top of Skaigh Wood. Follow the track as it bends to the right, then sharply to the left. Descend to the gate where your outward path initially forked (no 2) and turn right through it to go back along the firm track to Sticklepath and its Devonshire Inn.

The Devonshire Inn

4. South Zeal

Route: South Zeal – Stone Circle – Cordon Beacon – South Zeal

Distance: $7^1/_2$ miles

Map: O.S. Outdoor Leisure 28, Dartmoor

Start: The Oxenham Arms, South Zeal (Grid Reference SX 651935)

Access: South Zeal is beside the B3260 about five miles east of Okehampton. this walk starts in the centre of the village, which is served by bus no 51 from Okehampton and Exeter. The no 629 bus (Exeter -Okehampton – Bude) stops on the B3260 where this walk crosses the road.

The Oxenham Arms (0837 840244)

This is a very special pub. Apart from (maybe because of) the fact that a huge prehistoric standing stone is contained by the wall of the snug bar, it is famous for the story of the Oxenham family's white bird, as retold by Charles Kingsley in his book *Westward Ho!* The true facts of this story are detailed below. The pub also features in *John Herring* by the Reverend Sabine Baring-Gould and *The Beacon* by Eden Philpott. There are also legends of tunnels leading from the inn (perhaps folk memories of leys radiating from the standing stone). Lay monks built the place in the 12th century, although its first licence dates from 1477. Not long afterwards it became the Dower House (the window's share for life of a husband's estate) of the Oxenham family. Bed and breakfast accommodation is available, while real ale and food are served. Opening hours are 11 am to 2.30 pm and 6 pm to 11 pm on weekdays, noon to 3 pm and 7 pm to 10.30 pm on Sundays.

The White Bird

The white bird is an omen of death. It has been seen repeatedly over members of the Oxenham family shortly before they, often unexpectedly, die. The most famous instance is when the heiress Margaret Oxenham was about to marry Sir John of Roxamcowe. Her father saw the white bird hovering over her on the morning of her wedding but didn't tell her. When she came to stand before the altar, her rejected lover rushed up in mad desperation and stabbed her.

A printed account of 1641 includes drawings of the bird hovering over the death-beds of John Oxenham, two days before he died, aged 22, on 5th September 1635. he was followed on 7th September by Thomasine, his younger brother's wife, on 9th September, by his sister Rebecca, aged eight, and on 15th September by Thomasine's baby daughter. The same bird had appeared to John's grandmother Grace before she died in 1618. Witnesses to the apparition were examined at the behest of the Bishop of Exeter and found to be true.

Later, in 1743, the white bird was seen before the death of William Oxenham, while in December, 1873, there is a record that it appeared one week before the death of G.N. Oxenham, then the head of the family. It is not known if the bird appeared before the last member of the Oxenham family died in Canada in the early 1900s. Similarly, the White Birds of Salisbury Plain were seen to herald the deaths of the Bishops of Salisbury in 1885 and in 1911.

The Walk

1. Go right downhill, passing the post office on your right. At the bottom, turn right as signposted for the car park. pass this on your right and bear right at a fork to reach the B3260 near the bus stop for the no 629 service (Exeter – Okehampton – Bude). Cross this road to take the lane ahead, passing Newlyn Cottage on your right.

2. Fork left up an enclosed path which returns to the lane, now only very roughly surfaced, at a public path signpost. Keep to this main lane now, soon bearing right to a junction where you ignore the signposted path going to Beacon Cottage on your right but go ahead along the track which has two strips of concrete divided by a central strip of grass. Ignore the turning to Crowsnest, on your right, at the next signposted junction. Go ahead with the main track to pass through a gate. Ignore an opening in the wall on your left.

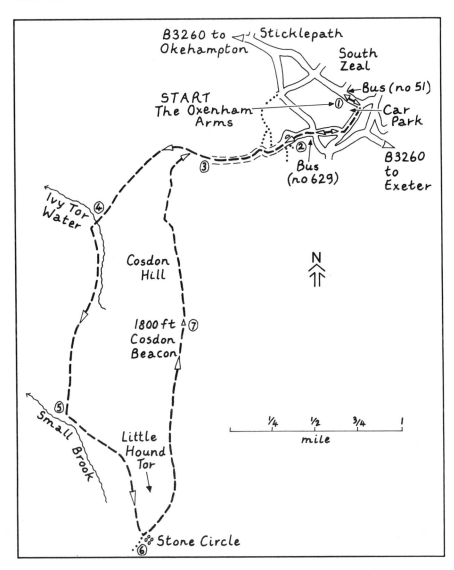

3. Reach the open moor and take the obvious track ahead (when it forks, keep right in the knowledge that the two branches will converge later). Ignore a faint path bearing uphill on your left (you will come down it). Keep the bulk of Cosdon Hill on your left as you follow the grassy track around it.

4. Cross Ivy Tor Water at a ford and bear left to walk parallel to the stream on your left. Continue along this path with Cosdon Hill on your left, to descend to another ford, in Small Brook.

5. Do not cross this ford! Bear left to walk upstream and gradually climb away from the stream. As you climb, bear gradually right and look for a stone circle on the plateau, near a T-junction formed by a path coming sharply from your left.

6. Facing the stone circle from the T-junction (i.e. looking approximately south), turn left along the sunken path, going roughly north-east. Soon bear northwards to reach the trig point and cairn at the 1800 foot high summit of Cosdon Beacon.

7. Go ahead, northwards, downhill to rejoin your outward track. Turn right along it to retrace your steps back to South Zeal and the Oxenham Arms.

The stone circle, south of South Zeal

5. Drewsteignton

Route: Drewsteignton – Fingle Bridge – Teign Gorge – Cranbrook Castle – Drewsteignton

Distance: 8 miles

Map: O.S. Outdoor Leisure 28 Dartmoor

Start: The Drewe Arms (Grid Reference SX 736908)

Access: Drewsteignton is on a minor road to the south of the A30 about 16 miles west of Exeter. Cars can be parked in the square, where buses stop from Exeter (no 359 every weekday) and Newton Abbot or Whiddon Down (no 671 on Wednesdays and Fridays).

The Drewe Arms (0647 21224)

This is a very special pub which seems as if it hasn't changed since the 16th century, although it was originally called the New Inn. After a spell as the Druids Arms it became the Drewe Arms when the Drewe family moved to the area just before the First World War. The landlady is the remarkable Mabel Mudge, in her nineties and affectionately known as 'Auntie'. She came to the inn when her husband Ernest (who died in 1971) became the landlord in 1919. Food isn't available (except lunchtime sandwiches if you're lucky) but real ale is served. Opening hours are 11 am to 2.30 pm and 6 pm to 11 pm on weekdays, noon to 3 pm and 7 pm to 10.30 pm on Sundays.

The Anglers Rest, Fingle Bridge (0647 21287)

Built in 1957, this pub follows in the tradition of the Old Mill, destroyed nearby by a fire in 1894. Mrs Jessie Ashplant, encouraged by the Rector of Drewsteignton, started selling teas here in the open air in 1897, then a tea shelter from 1907. Real ale and food, including a choice of at least five vegetarian dishes, are served. Opening hours are 11 am to 11 pm on weekdays, noon to 3 pm and 7 pm to 10.30 pm on Sundays.

Drewsteignton

Picturesque thatched cottages make Drewsteignton a much photographed village. The 15th century church stands near the pub, while the 20th century Castle Drogo is just down the road. Built by Sir Edwin Lutyens for Julius Drewe, the founder of Home and Colonial Stores, this became the last castle to be built in Britain when a 20 year task was completed in 1930. It is now in the care of the National Trust (open from April to October between 11 am and 6 pm, except on Fridays).

Fingle Bridge

Packhorses used this from the 16th century when a grainmill stood at the edge of the water and the woods provided charcoal. The Teign flows through a delightfully wooded gorge here. Come in late autumn and you may see salmon fighting their way up it to spawn. Herons may also be encountered.

The Walk

1. Go right, then left downhill to pass the bus shelter and bear right. Shortly after leaving the village, turn left along a path signposted to Fingle Bridge.

2. Turn left to walk along the path signposted to Fingle Bridge. This keeps near the edge of the wood and bears left at a signposted fork after 250 yards. Reach a road and turn right to follow it to The Anglers Rest, Fingle Bridge.

3. Do not cross Fingle Bridge. Take the signposted Fisherman's Path on your right. This goes upstream with the River Teign on your left and through delightful woodland. Reach a metal footbridge after one and a half miles.

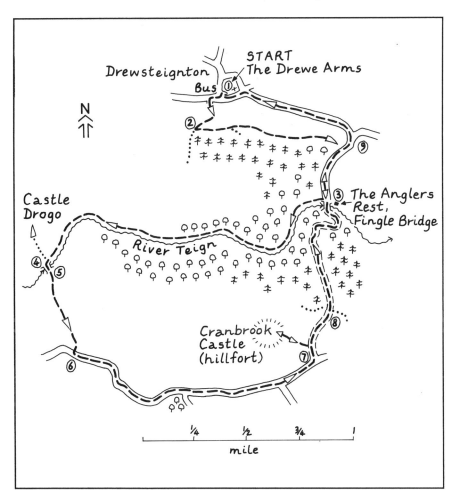

4. Turn left to cross the river by the metal footbridge. Take a stile over a stone wall and turn right along a wide track.

5. The path divides by another footbridge. Take the wide track which swings round to the left.

6. Go left when you come to a road. Ignore two right turnings as you follow this for over one mile. Climb to the top of a hill.

7. Turn left onto a wide track signposted for Fingle Bridge and Cranbrook Castle. The short detour up to the hillfort of Cranbrook Castle
   comes after about 100 yards, when the path leads off to the left.
   Returning to the wide track, resume walking northwards.

8. Keep to the wide track at a path junction. Bear left through the forest,
   as signposted to Fingle Bridge. Return past the Anglers Rest, on your
   right. Continue along the road.

9. Bear left when the road forks, to return to Drewsteignton and The
   Drewe Arms.

6. Chagford

Route: Chagford – Nattadon Common – Westcott Farm – Two Moors Way -Chagford

Distance: 4 miles

Map: O.S. Outdoor leisure 28 Dartmoor

Start: The Three Crowns Hotel (Grid Reference SX 701875)

Access: Chagford is at the end of the B3206 road, which runs for two miles westward from the A382 at Easton, about four miles south of this road's junction with the A30 at Whiddon Down. Bus no 359 runs on weekdays on its way between Whiddon Down and Newton Abbot on Wednesdays and Fridays. There is also the no 860 bus running between Moretonhampstead and Okehampton on Tuesdays, Wednesdays, Fridays and Saturdays.

The Three Crowns Hotel (0647 433444)

This is the most interesting of three popular pubs all within a couple of hundred yards of each other. The granite building dates from the 13th century when it was a manor house for John Whyddon and part served as a monks' hospice. It later became the dower house of the Whyddon family. It became a pub shortly after a black swan was added to the family crest by Queen Mary, in recognition of Judge Whyddon's services in the trial of the rebel Thomas Stafford. The pub was called The Black Swan and in 1641 it witnessed a scene which inspired R.D. Blackmore's novel *Lorna Doone*. Mary Whyddon (or Whiddon, as the family now spelled its name) was shot by a jealous lover as she entered the building from her wedding in nearby St Michael's Church. The pub's ghost is of the poet and Royalist Sidney Godolphin who was shot dead here by Roundheads after the battle at Bloody Meadow, to the east of Chagford. Bed and breakfast accommodation, food and real ale are all available at this pub, which is open between 11 am and 11 pm on weekdays, noon to 3 pm and 7 pm to 10.30 pm on Sundays.

The Globe Inn (0647 433485)

This 16th century coaching inn used to be called The Gregory's Arms. The pub is haunted by the ghost of a chambermaid who was accused of witchcraft. Her 'trial' was to be strapped in a chair and lowered into the river. She proved her innocence by being drowned! Jacket potatoes are a food speciality here, while real ale is also served. Bed and breakfast accommodation is available (stay in the Azalea Room to try and detect the ghost). Bar opening hours are 11 am to 3 pm and 6 pm to 11 pm on weekdays, noon to 3 pm and 7 pm to 10.30 pm on Sundays.

The Ring O'Bells (0647 432466)

This is the oldest of the three pubs, dating from 1177 (but the present building dates from the 16th century). It was linked with a nearby Christian shrine and provided shelter for pilgrims. The bell ringers in the nearby church were supplied with ale by this pub (charged to church funds) until the late 19th century. The stannary court was held here when Chagford was a stannary town. Prisoners were kept here before going to Okehampton Assizes. The mortuary used to be in an upstairs room at the back of the pub. Perhaps this accounts for the many tales of ghosts. Food and real ale are served, with bar opening hours being from 11 am to 3 pm and 6 pm to 11 pm on weekdays, noon to 3 pm and 7 pm to 10.30 pm on Sundays.

Chagford

When Chagford became a stannary town in 1305, along with Ashburton, Plympton and Tavistock, it meant that tin miners could bring their metal to be weighed, stamped and taxed here. there was also a thriving market for cattle and sheep (especially their wool). Later it became a tourist resort and was the home of James Perrott, the first Dartmoor Guide. One of his rambles led to Cranmere Pool (more accurately, a bog), where he had secreted a bottle. His Victorian clients were encouraged to leave their visiting cards in it to prove they had made the trek into the wilderness. This became the first of Dartmoor's 'letterboxes'. Now there are hundreds of them scattered around Dartmoor and you won't fail to meet people searching for them.

The Walk

1. Go right to pass the Globe Inn on your right and the church on your left. Turn right to walk south out of the village. Bear left into a small housing estate and reach a signpost for Nattadon Common.

2. Climb past a wood and with a wall on your left to the top of the common. Continue to a road and go right along it, ignoring another road which goes right at a T-junction.

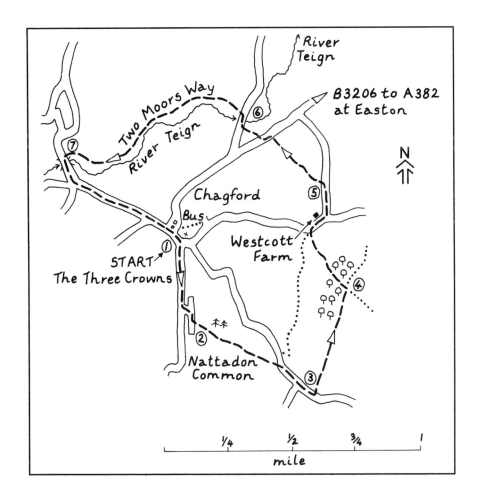

3. Turn left along the public footpath for Great Weeke and Yellam. Descend with a wall and hedge on your left, then along a narrow path and go through a gate into woodland.

4. Turn left at a path junction, cross a stile and head towards Westcott. Emerge over another stile onto a meadow. Take a third stile, on your left, cross a fourth stile and a stream and follow a track to a road. Bear right to pass Westcott Farm on your left. Bear left when the road forks to pass Adley House on your right.

5. Turn left along the public footpath which crosses two fields diagonally to reach houses and the B3206 road. Go left and leave the road almost immediately to take the public footpath to Ruchford Bridge. Turn right across the bridge.

6. Turn left along the public footpath to Chagford Bridge, keeping the River Teign on your left and walking upstream. Cross a footbridge over the tributary stream ahead. This path is part of the Two Moors Way.

7. Join the road to cross Chagford Bridge and take the road bearing left at a crossroads to return to Chagford. Pass the octagonal Market House which presides over the square on your left, opposite the Ring O'Bells pub, before returning to the Three Crowns Inn on your right.

The Three Crowns

7. Steps Bridge

Route: The Steps Bridge Inn – St Thomas Cleave Wood – The Steps Bridge Inn

Distance: $2^1/_2$ miles

Map: O.S. Outdoor Leisure 28 Dartmoor

Start: The Steps Bridge Inn (Grid Reference SX 804883)

Access: Steps Bridge is on the B3212 road between Exeter and Moretonhampstead. Bus no 359 provides a regular weekday service between Exeter and Moretonhampstead via Steps Bridge, while bus no 82 passes by on its journey between Exeter and Plymouth on certain days in the summer (all weekends from late May to mid September and daily during the school summer holidays).

The Steps Bridge Inn (0647 52313)

This modern pub has a wonderful setting beside the river and surrounded by trees. There is a beer garden, while bed and breakfast accommodation is available. Real ale and food are served, as are Devonshire

cream teas. The pub is closed on Tuesday and Wednesday evenings, otherwise the opening hours on weekdays are noon to 5 pm and 7.30 pm to 10.30 pm, with Sunday hours being noon to 3 pm and 7 pm to 10.30 pm.

St Thomas Cleave Wood

The early spring is the best time to visit the woodlands of the Teign Gorge. Witness a spectacular carpet of daffodils. Wild flowers are in abundance later in the year too. The National Trust attempts to keep visitors away from the flowers, so that they can be seen but not picked. Autumn brings a carpet of leaves, of course. Take care not to slip on the wooden footbridges at this season. Information on the wildlife is available in the Dartmoor National Park's Centre near the start of this walk. If you're lucky, you may see a kingfisher.

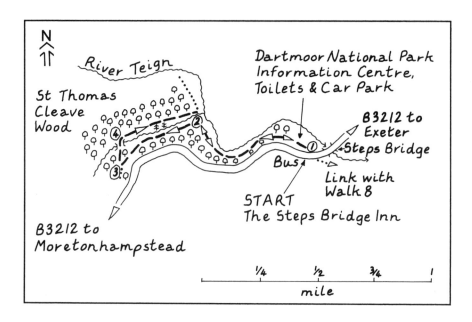

The Walk

1. Go right from the inn. Avoid the road by taking steps from the car park to a footbridge and more steps which lead to the Dartmoor national Park Information Centre. Continue along the signposted public footpath to St Thomas Cleave Wood, passing public toilets on your right. Go ahead over a stile or through the small wooden gate beside it and follow the fairly firm path through woodland, with meadows and the River Teign below on your right.

2. Reach a signposted path junction immediately before a footbridge over a tributary stream. Do not cross it. Do turn left up the signposted circular walk. This climbs steeply above the stream on your right.

3. Having climbed to a path junction, turn right down the signposted circular walk. Take a footbridge across the stream.

4. Turn right to walk downstream. A delightful wooded walk ensues with broadleaved trees clothing the slope on your left and a plantation of conifers shielding the stream on your right. Descend to another signposted path junction. Turn right to cross the footbridge and go ahead to retrace your steps to the Information Centre and the Steps Bridge Inn.

8. Dunsford

Route: Dunsford – Stepping Stones – Steps Bridge – Stepping Stones -Dunsford

Distance: $2^1/_2$ miles

Map: O.S. Pathfinder 1329 Topsham

Start: The Royal Oak Inn, Dunsford (Grid Reference SX 812892)

Access: Dunsford is near the B3212 between Exeter and Moretonhampsteam. Bus no 359 stops in the village on its way between Exeter and Moretonhampstead on weekdays. The seasonal no 82 bus between Exeter and Plymouth (all weekends from late May to mid September and daily during the school summer holidays) passes by on the B3212.

The Royal Oak Inn (0647 52256)

Belgian bottled beer is a speciality here, as are home made pies. Vegetarians have a choice of five dishes daily. The pub is a great favourite with walkers, while Screaming Lord Such has supped here (tasting the pub's 100th different guest real ale, which is now called 'Such Taste'). The pub's name reflects the loyalty of the local gentry to King Charles I. At the Restoration, Charles II planned to establish an Order of the Royal Oak. He had escaped capture by Cromwell's forces by hiding in an oak tree. Being part of the Fulford estate, the inn was given its name by the staunchly Royalist Sir Francis Fulford.

An inn had stood here since at least the 15th century but it was burnt down in 1887. The red-brick Victorian inn was built to replace it. Bed and breakfast accommodation is available and bar opening hours are 11.30 am to 2.30 pm and 6.30 pm to 11 pm from Mondays to Thursdays 11.30 am to 3 pm and 6 pm to 11 pm on Fridays and Saturdays, noon to 3 pm and 7 pm to 10.30 pm on Sundays.

The Royal Oak

Dunsford

This is an attractive village with whitewashed cob and thatch cottages. Cob is a mixture of mud and straw. Walk 11 in this book features the White Hart Hotel, Moretonhampstead and the story of Jonathan May, a farmer from Dunsford who was murdered on his way home. Jonathan May's grave is in the churchyard of St Mary's, Dunsford, next door to the Royal Oak Inn.

The Walk

1. Go right to take the elevated pavement past the school on your right. Turn left at the signposted road junction and left again soon afterwards, as signposted for Steps Bridge and Moretonhampstead.

2. Turn left over a stile to follow the signposted public footpath to Mill House. Walk with a hedge on your right. When you approach a

corner, turn right over another stile and bear left through the field to a gate beside a roadside signpost opposite the white buildings of the Dunsford Mills Country House Hotel. Cross the B3212 road with care and take the signposted public footpath which goes down the side of the hotel on your left to stepping stones across the River Teign. The footbridge on your left is private.

3. Cross the river and a subsequent meadow to reach a signposted junction with a track just inside woodland.

4. Turn right as signposted for Steps Bridge. Pass Woodcote Cottage on your right to walk between the wood on your left and its garden fence on your right. Continue through the wood along a path way marked with yellow arrows. Climb to a broader track and bear right down it. Fork right along a lower, narrower, footpath to walk above the river on your right. This delightful woodland path leads down to the B3212 road opposite the Steps Bridge Inn, where this route may be linked with Walk 7 to form a five mile circuit.

Take these stepping stones across the River Teign

5. Retrace your steps from the B3212 at Steps Bridge Inn. Notice the National Trust sign for Bridford Wood on your right but immediately turn left along the narrow footpath, signposted for Swannaford or Stepping Stones for Dunsford. Fork left with the waymarked path to pass Woodcote Cottage on your left and turn right along its access track to the signposted junction. Turn left to reach the stepping stones and cross the river. Emerge on the B3212 road at Dunsford Mills Country House Hotel. Do not take the signposted public footpath opposite. Go right to pass the hotel on your right.

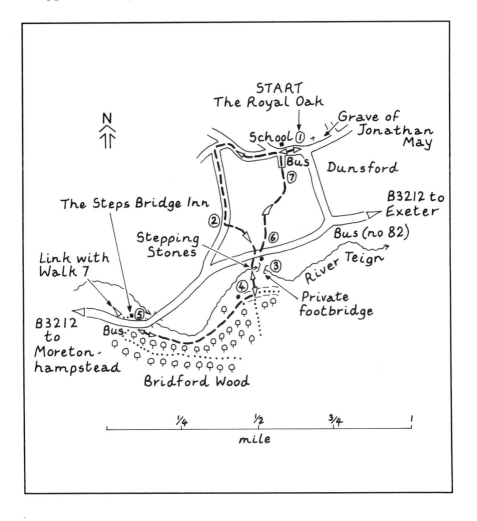

6. Immediately after passing Dunsford Mills Country House Hotel, turn left across the road and take the public footpath signposted for Dunsford Village. Cross a field diagonally to its far corner where a gap leads to the next field on your right. Continue with a hedge on your left. Bear left over a stile in the corner ahead and aim for the tower of Dunsford's church. Take the gap ahead and bear left over this field, with the church tower on your right.

7. Continue over a stile in the corner ahead. Follow an enclosed, narrow, footpath into the village. Reach the school and turn right along the elevated pavement back to the Royal Oak on your left. The church next door is worth a visit, if only to find the tombstone of Jonathan May (walk from the porch in the direction of the telephone box, away from the pub).

9. Lydford Gorge

Route: Lydford – White Lady Waterfall – Devil's Cauldron – Lydford

Distance: $3^1/_2$ miles

Map: O.S. Pathfinder 1327 Lydford

Start: The Castle Inn, Lydford (SX 510848)

Access: Oh, for the days when you could come by train to within a few yards of the White Lady Waterfall! At least there are still buses to Lydford, which is off the A386 between Tavistock and Okehampton. Bus no 118 runs on weekdays from Okehampton and from Tavistock (direct from Plymouth on Thursdays and Saturdays). Bus no 187 connects with trains from Plymouth at Gunnislake (Tamar Valley Line) on Sundays, when it also runs from Okehampton (and from Exeter – first bus out, last bus back).

The Castle Inn, Lydford (0822 82242 and 82252)

Dating back to the 16th century, this is one of the finest traditional inns in the West Country. Bed and breakfast accommodation is available in eight bedrooms, six of which are *en-suite* and one of which has a cherrywood four poster bed, ideal for a first or second honeymoon. The restaurant is recommended by Egon Ronay and features a vegetarian dish everyday. Bar meals are also available, as is real ale. There is a beer garden and the pub featured under the name of *The Admiral Blake* in the film *The Hound of the Baskervilles*. Bar opening hours are 11.30 am (noon on Saturdays) to 3 pm and 6 pm to 11 pm on weekdays, noon to 3 pm and 7 pm to 10.30 pm on Sundays.

Lydford

There are certain places which the traveller comes across without anticipation but which prove to be one of the truly magical spots. Lydford is one of them. Now a tiny village, devoid of its railway junction, it was

once one of the four important towns of Saxon Devon. Its name suggests
a more ancient origin and, indeed, its church is dedicated to the Celtic St
Petroc. He was a Welshman who studied in Ireland and landed in
Padstow, Cornwall, in the sixth century to set about building churches
and reviving the Faith. Petroc died in 564 and this church is said to date
from 641, so it may have been dedicated to him by later disciples. They
would probably have been Celtic, showing how this area of old Dumnonia survived until Ine and Nunna, the Saxon leaders of Wessex,
defeated the Celtic leader Geraint in 710. The church was rebuilt in the
Middle Ages. Notice the Watchmaker's Tomb near the porch. It is
inscribed thus:

'Here lies in Horizontal position
    The outside case of
    George Routleigh, Watchmaker,
Whose abilities in that line were an honour
    To his profession:
    Integrity was the main-spring,
    and Prudence the Regulator
    Of all the actions of his life:
    Humane, generous and liberal,
    His hand never stopped
    Till he had relieved distress;
So nicely regulated were all his movements
    That he never went wrong
    Except when set-a-going
    By People
    Who did not know
    His Key:
Even then, he was easily
    Set right again
He had the art of disposing of his Time
    So well,
    That his Hours glided away
    In one continual round
    Of Pleasure and Delight,
Till an unlucky Moment put a period to
    His existence;
    He departed this Life

November 14, 1802.
Aged 57,
Wound up,
In hopes of being taken in Hand
By his Maker
And of being
Thoroughly cleaned, repaired, and set-a-going
In the World to come'.

The church houses an exhibition on Lydford, which is the mother parish of Dartmoor and claims to be the largest parish in England. When fortifying Devon against Danish attacks, Alfred the Great, who reigned from 871 to 899, gave Lydford the same attention as Exeter, Barnstaple and Totnes. The remains of the Saxon defences, known as the Lydford Town Bank can be seen near the end of this walk. The original turf rampart, surmounted by a wooden palisade, was 40 feet wide. It was later faced with granite. Ethelred the Unready preferred to bribe the Danes with Dartmoor's silver. His Danegeld coins were minted here and specimens can be seen in the Castle Inn. The stone castle which

The Castle Inn

stands between the inn and the church was built in 1195. Its mound was part of an 11th century castle. Offenders against the Forest and stannary laws were imprisoned here. The stannary was the tinners' court and had an evil reputation. 'Lydford Law' was a byword for being sentenced without a proper trial. As the 17th century poet from Tavistock, William Browne, wrote:

'I oft have heard of Lydford Law,
How in the morn they hang and draw,
And sit in judgement after'.

Lydford Gorge

This spectacular gorge is, thanks to the National Trust, one of the best, most exciting, places to walk in England. Take care and hold onto the handrails when walking beside the river. The Gubbins family of fierce outlaws lived here in the 17th century, sleeping in holes, sharing everything including their women and stealing sheep from the moor. The gorge has a 100 foot waterfall where a White Lady is said to appear to anyone who falls in the river. The Devil's Cauldron is a pothole or rounded basin made by huge rocks that have been tossed around by the force of the water and ground against the river bed. Look for brown trout in the water and dragonflies and damselflies on the ring. The steepness of the gorge saved the oak woods about it. The pied woodpecker lives here, as do red deer. One of Britain's largest butterflies, the silver washed fritillary, may be seen, while shaggy ink cap fungi appear in late summer and autumn. Mosses, ferns and lichens thrive in the damp atmosphere near the Devil's Cauldron.

The Walk

N.B. The walk through Lydford Gorge is only possible between April and October (open daily, 10 am to 5 pm) and for an admission fee. The National Trust charged adults £2.80 (children £1.40) in 1993. The charge is a powerful incentive to join the National Trust and gain free admission (you can join the National Trust at the main entrance to Lydford Gorge, near direction point 2). The price of this walk also reflects the tremendous work done by the National Trust in providing safe access to what must rank as one of the most attractive gorges in England. It is well worth paying. This walk will live long in the memory.

1. Go right to pass Lydford Castle and St Petroc's Church on your right. There is a pavement on the left hand side of the road, which is followed across a bridge over the River Lyd. Reach the main entrance to the National Trust's Lydford Gorge on your right.

2. Turn right to enter Lydford Gorge and follow the National Trust's one-way system, necessary because of the popularity of this route and the need for careful single-file walking in places. Follow the path down to a gate, continue around a hairpin bend and reach a signposted junction. Bear left along the longer route to the Waterfall Entrance.

3. Cross a footbridge above the White Lady Waterfall (which will be seen later, from below). Reach a path junction, if you wish to link with walk 13 at the Manor Inn, go left. If you wish to complete this route, go right, as signposted for the White Lady Waterfall. Fork left at the next signpost to take the 'Long and Easy' path down to it. View the waterfall on your right and cross the footbridge on your left.

4. Follow the narrow but safe path upstream, with the River Lyd on your right. Ignore the first footbridge on your right. Take the second and go left, above the river on your left, to view the Devil's Cauldron. Don't proceed under the road bridge.

5. Retrace your steps from the Devil's Cauldron. Bear left to climb back to the main entrance and go left back into Lydford. Pass the Castle

Inn on your left and continue almost to the telephone box near the village hall. Notice the remains of Lydford's Saxon defences on your left. Retrace your steps and turn right along an enclosed and signposted path (to an ancient spring).

6. Go left at a path junction and reach the castle. Go left to return to the Castle Inn, Lydford.

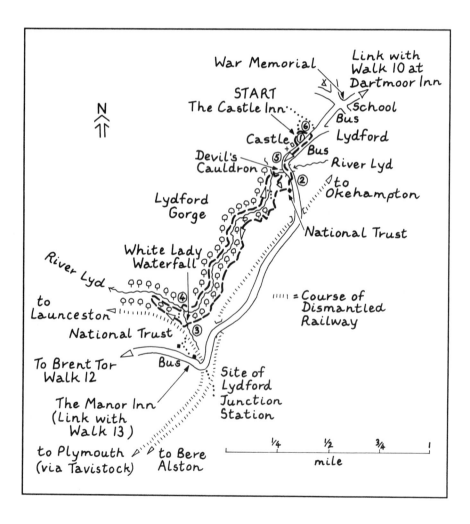

10. Widgery Cross

Route: Dartmoor Inn – Arms Tor – Widgery Cross – Dartmoor Inn

Distance: 3^1/^{2} miles

Maps: O.S. Pathfinder 1327, Lydford or O.S. Outdoor Leisure 28, Dartmoor

Start: Dartmoor Inn, Lydford (Grid Reference SX 523852)

Access: Dartmoor Inn is beside the A386 between Tavistock and Okehampton, at its junction with the road for Lydford. On Mondays, Fridays, Saturdays and Sundays it is possible to take the no 86 bus to here from either Barnstaple or Plymouth. Bus no 118 runs here every weekday from Okehampton and Tavistock (from Plymouth on Thursdays and Saturdays). A delightful way to come here on Sundays in July and August is on the no 187 bus which connects with trains from Plymouth at Gunnislake (Tamar Valley Line) and continues to Okehampton. The first no 187 bus out of Okehampton on Sunday mornings actually provides a service from Exeter, while the last bus into Okehampton on Sunday evenings allows for a return journey to Exeter.

Dartmoor Inn (0822 82221)

The 'King' of the notorious local Gubbins family was killed here and may be the ghost who throws glasses across the bar some evenings. The event is included in Charles Kingsley's *Westward Ho!*

Real ale and food are served but accommodation is no longer available. The inn dates back to at least the 16th century. Those of Drake's sailors and officers who lived in North Devon found it a convenient halfway house.

Widgery Cross

The tall granite cross
on the top of Brat Tor
(1511 foot above sea
level) was erected by
William Widgery in
1887. This Dartmoor
painter did so to com-
memorate Queen Vic-
toria's Golden Jubilee.
It is a glorious spot on
a fine day with views
over Lydford Gorge to
the south, with Ply-
mouth Sound in the
distance. The view of
the higher tors within
Dartmoor, to the east,
is also impressive.

Widgery Cross

The Walk

1. Go right to the road junction and turn right up a rough lane. Pass a
   house called 'Moorgate' on your right. Continue through a gate and
   along the signposted bridleway. Fork left, bearing away from the car
   park, towards Arms Tor, the left hand of two tors ahead. Walk with a
   wall surmounted by a fence on your left.

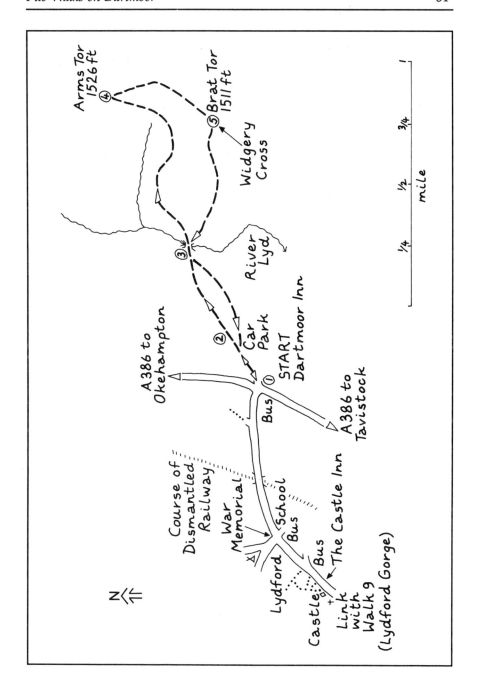

2. Go ahead through a gate and pass a bench placed in memory of Stuart Thayre (1951 – 86) on your left. Continue beside the wall on your left.

3. Take either the footbridge or the stepping stones across the River Lyd and follow the broad green track which bears gradually left before swinging back towards the col between the two tors ahead. Bear left when the drier ground is reached and attain the summit of Arms Tor.

4. Walk south towards Brat Tor, which is marked by Widgery Cross. Bear left to skirt above a marshy area at first.

5. Take the path which descends to the footbridge and stepping stones over the river. This time, fork left to take the grassy path to the car park. Cross a stile in the fence before it. Retrace your steps to the Dartmoor Inn.

11. Moretonhampstead

Route: Mortonhampstead – Butterdon Down – Moretonhampstead

Distance: 3 miles

Map: O.S. Outdoor Leisure 28 Dartmoor

Start: The White Horse, Moretonhampstead (Grid Reference SX 753860)

Access: Moretonhampstead is at the junction of the A382 and the B3312 about 12 miles west of Exeter. Buses nos 73 and 173 run every weekday from Newton Abbot. Bus no 82 runs on certain days (daily during the summer holidays) from Plymouth and Exeter, bus no 359 runs on weekdays from Exeter, bus no 671 runs from Whiddon Down and Newton Abbot on Wednesdays and Fridays only, while bus no 860 runs from Okehampton on Tuesdays, Wednesdays, Fridays and Saturdays only.

The White Horse (0647 40242)

This 17th century coaching inn was at one time known at the Grays Hotel, after the family who owned it. The original building was burnt down by a fire in 1838 for which help was sought from as far away as Exeter. Real ale and food are served, while bed and breakfast accommodation is available. Bar opening hours are 11 am to 11 pm on weekdays, noon to 3 pm and 7 pm to 10.30 pm on Sundays.

The White Hart Hotel (0647 40406)

This was a busy coaching inn before the railway came to Moretonhampstead in 1866 (from Newton Abbot). French officer prisoners of war were allowed to come here on parole from Dartmoor Prison during the Napoleonic Wars. Its position at a crossroads also led the Dartmoor Tinners' Great Court to hold their last meeting here in 1786. One unfortunate incident on record is the murder of Jonathon May, a farmer from Dunsford, on his way home from the fair at Moretonhampstead on

The White Hart

16th July 1835. He had unwisely shown off £80 while in this inn. His murderers were apprehended and sentenced to death. One, Thomas Oliver, went to the gallows after repenting and stating that the other, Edmund Galley, was innocent. Galley's sentence was commuted to transportation to Australia, from where in 1878 he was able to prove his innocence and receive £1,000 compensation – at the age of 80.

Moretonhampstead

Cross Street (going right from the two pubs featured here) was where the old Dancing Tree stood, near the almshouses. This ancient elm was where a band of French officers performed a concert in 1807. The present tree on the site is a copper beech, being planted after a snowstorm and gale caused the demise of the original in 1903. R. D. Blackmore wrote about 'most lively and dissipated' festivities that used to take place here in his novel *Christowell*.

The Walk

1. Go right to pass the White Hart Hotel on your right, then turn left around The Square and go down Ford Street. Follow its pavement past the hospital on your right. Reach Moretonhampstead's road sign (twin town Betton).

2. Turn right along the lane signposted to Howton. Ignore the turning to Howton which comes very soon on your left. Go ahead, as signposted to Butterton. Pass the entrance to Holcombe House Retirement Home on your right.

3. Turn left over a stone stile between two fieldgates. Follow the signposted public footpath (to Finglebridge via Butterdon) diagonally across the field to a wooden step stile in the far corner. Continue over it and keep a hedge on your left as you go ahead over three more stiles and reach a lane.

4. Do not take the fieldgate opposite! Bear right across the lane to take the public footpath signposted for Cranbrook and Fingle Bridge. This begins by going over a stile and keeps beside a hedge on your left. There is a conifer plantation on your right. Emerge over another stile to follow the left hand edge of a field. Take a stile in the corner, walk parallel to the hedge on your left and cross another waymarked stile. Continue with the hedge on your left over two more stiles.

5. Turn right along the signposted bridlepath to the road near Butterdon, passing along the foot of the Down on your left. Pass through a gate and by a house on your left. Turn right along the road for 250 yards, until it bends right.

6. Go ahead along a firm, hedged, track which is the signposted public footpath to Moreton. Keep left at the next signpost to pass Hill Farm Cottages on your right. Plunge down a steep path, go ahead through a gate and walk with a stream on your left and woodland on your right.

7. Don't take the gate ahead at the end of a small meadow. Bear right to cross a stile in the corner and turn left along a path just inside the wood. Emerge over a stile and go ahead beside a hedge on your left. Cross a stile in the next corner.

8. Bear right over a stile signposted to Queens Road. Follow the right hand edges of two fields then go down a hedged track to Queens Road. Ignore another road on your left. Go ahead down to the A382 road and turn left along its pavement to pass the hospital again and retrace your steps into Moretonhampstead.

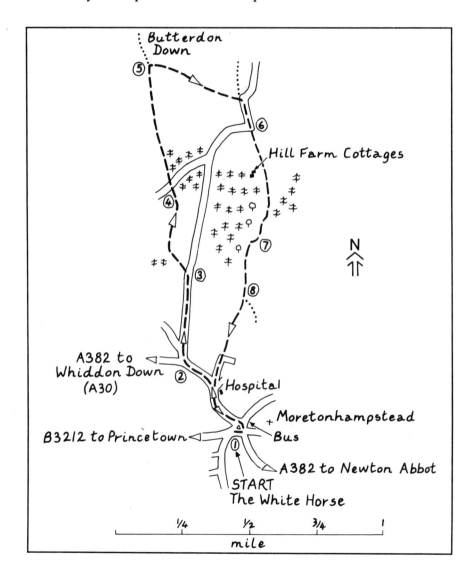

12. Brent Tor

Route: The Brentor Inn – North Brentor – Cattle Grid on the A386 for link with Walk 13 – South Brentor – St Michael's Church – The Brentor Inn

Distance: 7 miles

Map: O.S. Pathfinder 1327 Lydford

Start: The Brentor Inn (Grid Reference SX 472810)

Access: Buses nos 118 (on weekdays from Tavistock and Okehampton) and 187 (on Sundays in July and August from Okehampton and Gunnislake, connecting with trains from Plymouth) run to North Brentor. Ask if they will pass the Brentor Inn. Motorists will find it on a minor road between Tavistock and Lydford.

The Brentor Inn (0822 810240)

Dating from about 1700, this old coaching inn used to be called the Herring Arms, after a former landlord called Phil Herring. Perhaps they shouldn't have changed the name because his ghost now haunts the place. This friendly establishment serves excellent food, including vegetarian dishes. Bar snacks are available, as is real ale. Bed and breakfast accommodation is also here. Opening hours are 11 am to 2.30 pm and 6 pm to 11 pm on weekdays, noon to 3 pm and 7 pm to 10.30 pm on Sundays.

St Michael's Church, Brentor

This church wasn't built for the convenience of the parishioners. It stands on an exposed tor at 1095 foot above sea level because it is meant to be in a special spot. The dedication to St Michael (in this case St Michael de Rupe, or of the Rock) gives a clue. The official church guide even concedes that 'St Michael's on the Mount at Glastonbury is reputedly linked to St Michael's at Brent Tor by a ley line'. Indeed it is, the greatest such line in England, known as the Dragon Line and described in *The New View Over Atlantis* by John Michell (and in *The Sun and the Serpent* by Hamish Miller and Paul Broadhurst). As well as visiting Glastonbury Tor, this ley links Mount's Bay in Cornwall with the Cheesewring on Bodmin Moor, the church and former cathedral at Crediton, Avebury and Bury St Edmunds. The line can be drawn on the map but it can also be dowsed. Coming to Brent Tor, I dowsed around the church in gale conditions, demanding that my dowsing rods only cross at the Dragon Line. They did (I suspect other leys converge here too) and my compass showed the direction was approximately 60° (conditions were too bad for exact measurement). Transferring this compass bearing to the map within the shelter of the church I found that this was the right direction (within the church the ley goes diagonally between the corner to the left of the altar as you face it to the far opposite corner).

Brent Tor

The Walk

1. Go left down the road and turn right along the road for Brentor and Mary Tavy. Turn right at the war memorial to pass Christ Church on your left. Continue past Brentor's old railway station on your right. Go ahead over a cattlegrid.

The old railway station, Brentor

2. Turn left and immediately fork right on the higher road, above the houses but at the foot of the moor. When the road bends left downhill, turn right uphill and keep the 1158 foot summit of Gibbet Hill on your left. Reach the A386 at the roadsign for Mary Tavy (twinned with Mery-Corbon), near a cattle grid.

3. Either link here with Route 13 (Wheal Betsy) or continue this route by bearing right up a moorland track. Twice be sure to fork right on the higher path. The 1158 foot summit of Gibbet Hill is away to your right and Brent Tor comes into view ahead.

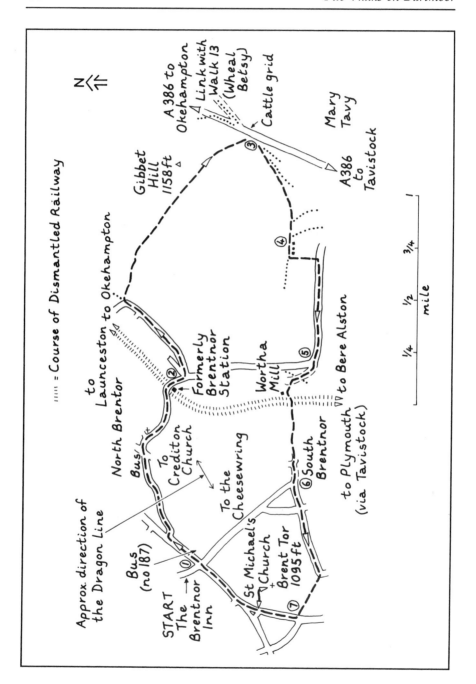

..... = Course of Dismantled Railway

4. Join a track at houses on your left and turn left with it down to a road. Go right along this road, towards Brent Tor.

5. When the road bends right, fork left down a No Through Road. Descend past the 'unsuitable for motors' sign and over a cattle grid. Sharp bends lead to the ruins of Wortha Mill. Go ahead over two bridges across the two old railway lines and take the old green lane ahead to South Brentor.

6. Go ahead along a lane, ignoring lanes on your right. Pass Coles Cottage on your left, then Brennen Cottage. Go ahead 150 yards to where the lane turns left. Bear right through a gate to follow a signposted bridlepath which runs beside a hedge on your left and below Brent Tor on your right. Reach a road at a signpost.

7. Go right along the road. Divert right up the path to St Michael's Church. Return to the road and go right again to return to the Brentor Inn.

13. Wheal Betsy

Route: The Mucky Duck, Lydford – Wheal Betsy Engine House – Wheal Jewell Reservoir – The Mucky Duck, Lydford

Distance: $5^1/_2$ miles

Maps: O.S. Outdoor Leisure 28 Dartmoor, O.S. Pathfinder 1327 Lydford

Start: The Mucky Duck, Lydford (Grid Reference SX 502832)

Access: The Mucky Duck, was extremely convenient for the old railway junction. Now it can, at least, be reached by bus (no 118 on weekdays from Tavistock or Okehampton and no 187 on Sundays in July and August from Okehampton or Gunnislake, where a connection is made with the train from Plymouth). Motorists should turn off the A386 at the Dartmoor Inn (between Tavistock and Okehampton) and follow the minor road through Lydford.

The Mucky Duck, Lydford (0822 82208)

The hotel which served the railway has survived it. Bed and breakfast accommodation is available, while the Mucky Duck Bar is popular. Real ale and food are served. Vegetarian dishes are always on the menu, while there is a beer garden and a family area. Opening hours are 11 am to 11 pm on weekdays, noon to 3 pm and 7 pm to 10.30 pm on Sundays. The pub has four ghosts, being a Mrs Matthews, two young children and a teenage girl. They are often seen and heard by bar staff.

Wheal Betsy

This is the best surviving engine house on Dartmoor. Begun in 1806 and reopened in 1863 under the new name of The Prince Arthur Consols, this mine produced silver and lead until the 1870s.

Lydford Junction Station

The originally broad gauge Launceston and South Devon Railway met the London and South Western Railway's line from Okehampton to Bere Alston (also for Plymouth) here. The former was closed in 1962 (it opened in 1865) while the latter (*which had opened in 1890*) survived until 1968.

Riders from Cholwell pass the engine house of Wheal Betsy

The Walk

1. Go left to take the road across the old railway (from Launceston) and turn right along a signposted public bridleway immediately after the bridge. Bear left to pass above the Classical Riding Academy and cross the bridge over the old railway from Okehampton. Bear left to a gate in the corner, take it and be sure to shut it (a sign states 'Penalty for not shutting gate £2').

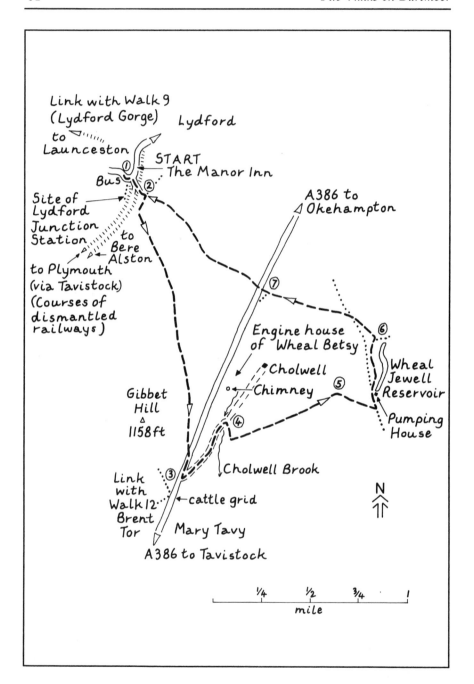

Link with Walk 9
(Lydford Gorge)   Lydford
to
Launceston
① Bus
② START
The Manor Inn

Site of
Lydford
Junction
Station
to
Bere
Alston
to Plymouth
(via Tavistock)
(Courses of
dismantled
railways)

A386 to
Okehampton

⑦

Engine house
of Wheal Betsy

⑥

Wheal
Jewell
Reservoir

Cholwell
Chimney

⑤

Pumping
House

Gibbet
Hill
△
1158ft

④

Cholwell Brook

Link
with
Walk 12
Brent
Tor

③

←cattle grid

N
⇑

Mary Tavy

A386 to Tavistock

¼   ½   ¾   ·   1
mile

2. Turn right to walk beside a fence on your right for 200 yards then bear left along a grassy track through bracken. Go ahead at a crosspaths and bear very slightly right as you climb the exposed moorland, with Brent Tor on the horizon away to your right. Keep the 1158 foot summit of Gibbet Hill on your left as you descend to the A386 road. Go right for about 300 yards to where the access lane for the signposted Cholwell Farm and Riding Stables comes up sharply from your left.

3. If you wish to link this route with No 12 (Brent Tor) go ahead to the cattle grid near the road sign for Mary Tavy (twinned with Mery-Corbon). Continue this route by turning sharply left down Cholwell Farm and Riding Stables' access lane. See the chimney of Wheal Betsy's engine house ahead, then turn right with the lane to cross Cholwell Brook.

4. Turn right to follow the signposted bridlepath to the rim of the valley, then bear left with its stony track to reach a gate in the fence near another signpost for the bridlepath. Maintain your direction, aiming just to the left of a belt of trees on the horizon and converge with a wall on your right. Keep the wall on your right and reach where it turns right to form a corner.

5. Bear slightly right to reach a firm track. Turn left along it to pass the pumping house for Wheal Jewell Reservoir, which is also passed on your right.

6. Fork left at the end of the reservoir. Bear left at the next fork to take a track which reaches the A386 road just to the left of where a power line crosses it (to join the power line running parallel to the road).

7. Cross the road carefully and go ahead in the company of the power line down to the gate with the notice about a £2 fine if you don't shut it. Take it to retrace your steps to the Manor Inn.

14. Peter Tavy

Route: Peter Tavy – Boulters Tor – Horndon – Mary Tavy – Peter Tavy

Distance: $5^1/_2$ miles

Maps: O.S. Pathfinders 1327 Lydford and 1340 Tavistock

Start: The Peter Tavy Inn (Grid Reference SX 512777)

Access: Peter Tavy is at a junction of minor roads east of the A386 about three miles north of Tavistock. Bus no 118 passes nearby along the A386 on weekdays, while bus no 187 follows a similar route between Tavistock and Okehampton on Sundays. The best day to come by bus is on a Friday, when there is a bus (no 95) direct to Peter Tavy from Tavistock.

The Peter Tavy Inn (0822 810348)

This 15th century pub is full of character. It is close to the church and one vicar was keen to ensure that nobody was in the pub drinking during services. He used to send his churchwarden to check, but the warden was also a relative of the publican. He therefore kept his eyes on the ground and walked slowly to the pub saying 'I'm coming, Cousin Tom, I'm coming, Cousin Tom'. This gave the drinkers time to hide and the warden the ability to report back that he had seen nobody drinking during the service. When Frank 'Axeman' Mitchell escaped from Princetown Prison he is said to have visited the inn. The notorious Kray twins settled his account with a cheque that used to be attached to a wooden ceiling beam behind the bar. Real ale and food are available and the opening hours are 11.30 am to 2.30 pm (3 pm on Saturdays) and 6.30 pm to 11 pm during the week, noon to 3 pm and 7 pm to 10.30 pm on Sundays.

The Elephant's Nest, Horndon (0822 810273)

This was called the New Inn until 1952 when an overweight landlord was told he looked like 'an elephant on his nest'. One wall has a mural depicting five elephants. There is also a large collection of china elephants. Exotic bank notes are also on display. Bed and breakfast accommodation is available, while real ale and food are served. Opening hours are 11.30 am to 2.30 pm and 6.30 pm to 11 pm on weekdays, noon to 3 pm and 7 pm to 10.30 pm on Sundays.

Peter Tavy

There are abandoned copper, lead and tin mines in this area. its sister village, Mary Tavy boasts the bones of William Crossing, the famous writer on Dartmoor, at the top of its churchyard. His *Guide* was published by *The Western Morning News* in 1909 while a series of Crossing's newspaper articles was published in bookform as *Crossing's Dartmoor Worker* in 1966. They depict the lives of workers such as the peat-cutter, the wallbuilder and the miner, as well as writing about visitors and artists.

The Walk

1. Bear left along the lane and turn right at a junction. Continue to the Post Office and bear left along the bridleway signposted for Combe.

2. Go left across the bridge and climb past Combe Cottages. Walk above a stream on your right but don't cross it. Turn left to reach a gate and signpost near a farm.

3. Go right to follow a track and bear left at a fork.

4. A stony track leads around Boulters Tor. Turn left to follow a grassy path with a wall on your right. Go through a fieldgate and descend beside a wall on your left. Cross a bridge over a stream and bear left along a lane.

5. Go right along a road for about a quarter of a mile then turn left to follow the signposted public footpath through a field. Bear right to descend to the River Tavy and cross a bridge to follow a stony track back into Horndon.

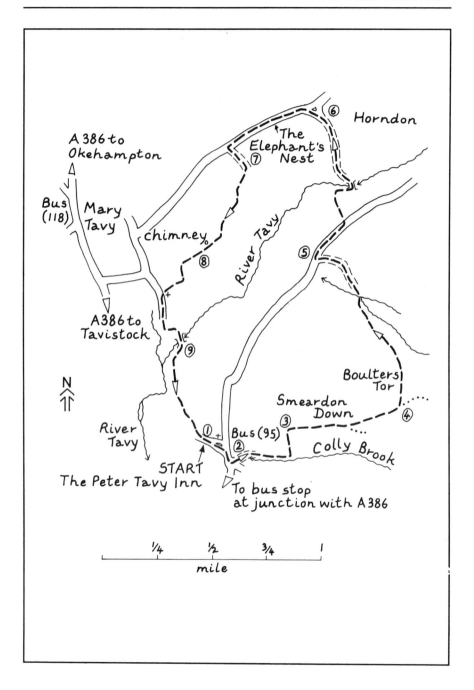

6. Fork left and go left along the Mary Tavy road to pass the Elephant's Nest Inn on your left. About a quarter of a mile after it, turn left along a track.

7. Continue along fieldpaths and descend, as signposted to an old mine whose chimney has survived.

8. Cross a ladder stile to descend and turn left to reach a gate on your right. Go ahead to Mary Tavy church, taking a stone step stile into the churchyard. Reach a lane and go left. Continue as a track and cross a bridge over the River Tavy.

9. Follow the signposted bridlepath for Peter Tavy, where the Peter Tavy Inn is on your left as you enter the village.

The Peter Tavy Inn

15. Hound Tor

Route: The Kestor Inn, Manaton – Becka Falls – Hound Tor – The Kestor Inn, Manaton

Distance: 6 miles

Map: O.S. Outdoor Leisure 28 Dartmoor

Start: The Kestor Inn, Manaton (Grid Reference SX 757807)

Access: Manaton is on a minor road about five miles south of Moreton-hampstead. There is a bus (no 671) which runs between Whiddon Down and newton Abbot on Wednesdays and Fridays, while there is a bus (no 171) on summer Sundays from Newton Abbot.

The Kestor Inn, Manaton (0572 85204)

This is the headquarters of the M.C.C. (Manaton Cricket Club, of course!). It has only been the village pub since the early 20th century. There used to be an inn (the Half Moon) on Manaton village green but the landlord closed it down in favour of this building which he'd had built as a boarding house for farm labourers. The granite used in its construction came from near Kestor Rocks, Chagford. There is a delightful children's play area beside the beer garden. Real ale and food are served, while bed and breakfast accommodation is available. Opening hours are 11 am to 2.30 pm and 6.30 pm to 11 pm on weekdays, noon to 3 pm and 7 pm to 10.30 pm on Sundays.

Becka Falls

These cataracts are located in natural woodland and are extremely popular during the tourist season.

Hound Tor

This is the tor which inspired Sir Arthur Conan Doyle to write about the local legendary phantom hounds from hell in *The Hound of the Basker-villes*. Sir Hugo Baskerville may have been based on the evil local Sir Richard Cabell, who died in 1677.

The Kestor Inn, Manaton

The Walk

1. Go left along the Road for Becky Falls and Bovey Tracey, immediately ignoring a lane to Water on your left. At the end of the village, bear left with the signposted public footpath to Becky Falls. This goes through a gate and alongside woodland on your right. Continue through the woods. Ignore a blue waymark post (for the A Trail) on your right. Reach a signpost near a footbridge.

2. Go ahead, as signposted, to The Falls. Bear right to see them from their base, then retrace your steps to the footbridge. Go left across it and take the path which bears right to pass a restaurant, gift and craft shop on your left. This brings you to a road opposite the car park. Go

right to a road junction and turn sharply left, as for Beckaford. Ignore
the private drive to Leighton House on your right, then the lane
going to Beckaford Farm on your left. Go over a cattle grid to open
moorland.

3. Turn right uphill to walk with a wall on your right up to a track.
   Turn right along this to skirt Black Hill on your left.

4. Ignore another track going right. Go ahead to walk with a wall on
   your right. Bear right at a public bridleway signpost, for Houndtor
   Down.

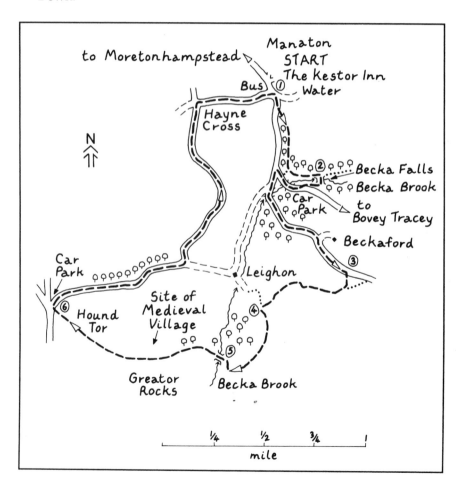

5. Cross the stone footbridge over Becka Brook and go ahead to pass Greator Rocks, the remains of a medieval village and the piles of rocks on Hound Tor. Reach a road opposite a car park.

6. Turn right along the road and descend to pass a No Through Road to Leighon on your right, as your road bends left towards Manaton. Reach the crossroads at Hayne Cross (where Sandy Meadow is the house name on your left) and turn right to follow the lane back to the bus stop at the Post Office on the main road immediately below the Kestor Inn.

16. Tavistock

Route: The Ordulph Arms, Tavistock – The Meadows – Drake's Statue -Cricket Ground – Whitchurch Down – The Ordulph Arms, Tavistock

Distance: 5 miles

Map: O.S. Pathfinder 1340 Tavistock

Start: The Ordulph Arms, Tavistock (Grid Reference SX 481745)

Access: Tavistock is about 13 miles north of Plymouth, where the A386 meets the A390 and the A384. Buses that run to its bus station include nos 83, 84 and 84A from Plymouth (daily service), no 118 from Oke-hampton on weekdays and no 187 from Okehampton and Gunnislake (for trains to Plymouth) on Sundays in July and August.

The Ordulph Arms (0822 615048)

This pub is easily reached from Tavistock's Bedford Square. Go up Drakes Road and turn left at Kilworthy Hill. it is named after the founder of the Benedictine Abbey in Tavistock in 974. It didn't become a pub until shortly before the start of World War II but it was once a temperance hotel. Part of its building is an archway that served as the gatehouse of the Glanville family's town house. Charles I spent the night here in 1644. Real ale is served, while the food is home-made and delicious. Bar opening hours are 11 am to 3 pm and 5 pm to 11 pm on weekdays, noon to 3 pm and 7 pm to 10.30 pm on Sundays.

Tavistock

Tavistock is the market town for the western part of Dartmoor. There is a Victorian market on Wednesdays, the Pannier Market (first held in 1105) on Fridays and an antique and craft market on Tuesdays. The town began as a Saxon camp ('stock') beside the River Tavy in the 8th century. This was when Saxon Devon was emerging out of the old Celtic kingdom of Dumnonia. By 974 their rule was well established and

Ordulf, a relative of the King of Wessex and Mercia, built a great abbey here. It was burnt down by the Danes in 997. Rebuilt on an even grander scale, it became the wealthiest in South West England. Very little has survived the Dissolution of 1539, although the 12th century Court Gate at Bedford Square was the main entrance to the abbey. Tavistock became a Stannary Town in 1281, recognising its importance as a centre for miners on western Dartmoor. Ingots of tin were brought here for weighing, assaying and stamping. Cloth was the chief local product by the 17th century but copper mining brought the development of a canal of four miles to carry the ore to the River Tamar at Morwellham in the early 19th century. Engineered by John Taylor, it was cut largely by French prisoners of war. When the railway linked Tavistock to Plymouth in 1859, it served 156 active copper mines. Most were closed by 1900 and both this old G.W.R. line and the London & South West Railway's line, which reached Tavistock in 1892 from Okehampton, were shut in the 1960s. The Duke of Bedford made a fortune out of the copper mines and rebuilt the town centre in the mid 19th century. The statue to Tavistock's most famous son, Sir Francis Drake, was erected in 1883 and is the original by Boehm from which the replica on Plymouth Hoe is taken.

The cricket ground, Tavistock; note the standing stones marking the boundary

The Walk

1. Go ahead down North Street. Take the zebra crossing to St Eustachius' Church. Follow the footway past the church on your left to reach Plymouth Road. Turn right along its pavement and take another zebra crossing to reach the opposite side. Maintain your direction along this pavement to pass the bus station over the road on your right.

2. Turn left when level with another zebra crossing and follow a path past tennis courts on your right and over a bridge ahead. Turn right to walk with a canal on your right and the Meadows on your left. Ignore another footbridge on your right, reach a road bridge and go right to cross it and see the statue of Sir Francis Drake.

3. Retrace your steps over the bridge and back into the Meadows. Turn right to walk from the canal to the River Tavy. Go left to walk upstream with the river on your right. Turn right over a footbridge and continue to a road. Bear left uphill and go under an old railway bridge.

4. Go right, uphill, at a T-junction. Pass Westwood Veterinary Centre on your left, then Westmoor Park. Turn left up Whitham Park. Take the wooden gate at the top of this road to enter the park. Go ahead to pass the cricket ground (with the boundary marked by standing stones – is this the biggest stone circle in the world?) on your left. Continue through the golf course to enter the official area of Dartmoor national Park on Whitchurch Down.

5. Pass the cricket ground on your left as you return through the parkland to Tavistock. Go through a kissing-gate in the bottom right hand corner and take the path to Down Road.

6. Pass Downlea on your left and descend with the pavement to a junction. Turn left to the Market Inn and go right to retrace your steps under the railway bridge and over the footbridge. Turn right to walk upstream with the River Tavy on your right.

7. Pass a swimming pool on your left, then the weir in the river on your right before joining a road near the Post Office. Go left to Bedford Square and take Drakes Road ahead. Turn left into Kilworthy Hill to return to the Ordulph Arms.

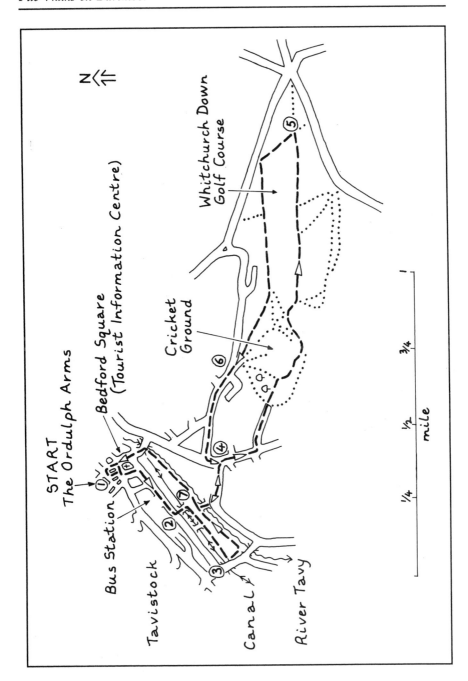

17. Merrivale

Route: Dartmoor Inn, Merrivale – Stone Rows – Dismantled Railway – Ingra Tor – Ward Bridge – Sampford Spinney – Dartmoor Inn, Merrivale

Distance: 7 miles

Maps: O.S. Pathfinder 1340, Tavistock or O.S. Outdoor Leisure 28, Dartmoor

Start: Dartmoor Inn, Merrivale (Grid Reference SX 549752)

Access: Merrivale is on the B3357 between Tavistock and Princetown. Buses nos 98 and 98A link these two towns on weekdays, while there is a Sunday service (no 170) which runs between Tavistock and Newton Abbot in July and August.

Dartmoor Inn, Merrivale (0822 890340)

Travellers have been the mainstay of this pub since stage coaches ran this way (note the guide stone on the walk, erected around 1700 for travellers between Tavistock and Ashburton). At the end of the 19th century the place was also alive with quarrymen. (Merrivale still has a working quarry). The Bishops Way was proclaimed here on the first Sunday of March, 1950, when a way was made 'where there was none before ...to the further upholding of the democratic way of life'. The place is also haunted. One ghost is of a young girl who died around 1900 and now walks through doors off the upstairs corridor. Why not stay overnight here on a bed and breakfast basis to see if she'll visit you? Camping may also be possible. Food and real ale are available and the bar opening hours are 11 am to 3 pm and 6 pm to 11 pm on weekdays, noon to 3 pm and 7 pm to 10.30 pm on Sundays.

Stone Rows

These baffle the archaeologists, who can only refer to them as 'ceremonial monuments'. A stone circle is nearby, as are prehistoric hut circles. The stone rows catch the eye, however. Two double rows of stones run parallel to each other from west to east. The northern one is about 200 yards long, while the southern is about 290 yards long. Both are terminated by a stone blocking the eastern end. In other cultures, we might be discussing spirit paths. They date from the Bronze Age.

A stone row, Merrivale

Vixen Tor is named after Vixana. Legend tells that she was a witch who made her home here and conjured up mists so that travellers were caught in the bogs. She was finally pushed to her death from the top of the tor.

The Walk

1. Go left along the B3357 road and cross the bridge over the River Walkham. Continue until the wall on your right turns to climb up into the moor and there is a waymark stone. Bear half right over the moor to pass above a car park on your left and reach prehistoric hut circles preceding two stone rows on your right.

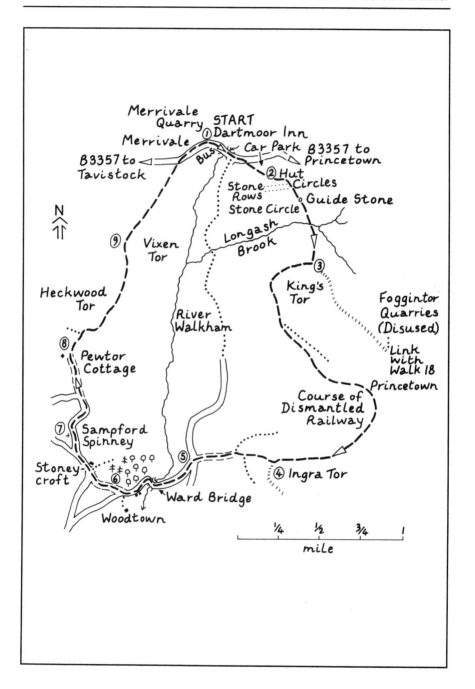

2. Walk to the eastern ends of the stone rows and bear right towards a tall guide stone, erected about 1700 and with the letters T (for Tavistock) and A (for Ashburton) on the respective faces. The television mast on top of North Hessary Tor rises behind it. Turn right to descend to cross the Longash Brook and climb towards King's Tor beside a wall on your right.

3. Reach the course of the dismantled Princetown railway and turn right to follow it around the western side of King's Tor. Follow the old railway for two miles, going round a sweeping curve above a valley on your right. The rocks of Ingra Tor are just above on your left.

4. As the railway bends to the left around Ingra Tor, descend on your right to join a wall on your left and take the lane ahead to a crossroads.

5. Go ahead along the road for Ward Bridge and Woodtown. Descend steeply to Ward Bridge, then climb with the road as it bears sharply left. Pass the cottages of Ward Bridge. Go ahead 100 yards.

6. Bear right over a cattle grid to follow a walled green lane. Keep with a stone wall on your right as you pass Stoneycroft. Fork right to pass Sampford Spinney's church on your left.

7. Bear right with the road, then left. As the road is about to bear left again, fork right up a track to Pewtor Cottage.

8. Continue along a grassy track and go round a corner made by walls on your right. Follow this track past Heckwood Tor (on your left) and Vixen Tor (on your right).

9. Go straight ahead when the wall turns right. The wall curves back to rejoin your path. Walk with it on your right to the B3357 and go right along this road back to the Dartmoor Inn, Merrivale, on your left.

18. Princetown

Route: Princetown – Foggintor Quarries – North Hessary Tor Television Mast – Princetown

Distance: 7 miles

Maps: O.S. Pathfinder 1340, Tavistock or O.S. Outdoor Leisure 28, Dartmoor

Start: The Prince of Wales Inn, Princetown (Grid Reference SX 589736)

Access: Princetown is at the junction of the B3357 and the B3212, about eight miles east of Tavistock. Buses nos 98 and 98A connect it with Tavistock on weekdays, while during July and August there is a bus (no 170) running on Sundays between Tavistock and Newton Abbot. Bus no 82 links Princetown with Plymouth and Exeter on weekends throughout the summer and daily during the school summer holidays.

The Prince of Wales (0822 890219)

Built in 1854, this is a very welcoming pub. The landlord is just one of many witnesses of a ghost, who may be a former landlord who shot himself. Bed and breakfast accommodation is available, as are food and real ale. Opening hours are 11 am to 3 pm and 6.30 pm to 11 pm on weekdays, noon to 3 pm and 7 pm to 10.30 pm on Sundays.

The Plume of Feathers Inn (0822 890240)

There is an Alpine bunkhouse here, as well as a camping area and ordinary bed and breakfast accommodation. Real ale, food (including vegetarian meals), a beer garden, a family room, an adventure playground and a skittle alley are all available. Built in 1785, this inn really welcomes walkers, but ladies beware! A ghostly presence haunts the ladies toilets. Opening hours are 11 am to 11 pm on weekdays, noon to 3 pm and 7 pm to 10.30 pm on Sundays.

Princetown

The High Moorland Visitor Centre was opened in the former Duchy Hotel in the centre of Princetown on 9th June, 1993. Open daily between 10 am and 5 pm with free admission, it is an essential place for all tourists on Dartmoor to visit. Its exhibitions are very impressive and informative.

It was appropriate that Prince Charles should perform the opening ceremony because it was the patronage of an earlier Prince of Wales that led to the creation of this small town at such an exposed spot, 1300 foot above sea level.

It is used to dealing with visitors, having a captive market in Dartmoor prison. The prison is here because of Princetown, not the other way around, however. In 1785 a friend of the then Prince of Wales, a Lord Warden of the Stannaries and a Secretary of the Duchy of Cornwall, Thomas Tyrwitt, had the vision of improving the 'useless waste' of Dartmoor to grow crops and provide good grazing. The Plume of Feathers Inn (referring to the Prince of Wales) was built to cater for a small community set to improve the land and communications. Tyrwitt failed to appreciate the severity of the local climate, so when the Napoleonic Wars brought the need to find a place to house the French prisoners, he built a prison here. American prisoners of war were also kept here as a result of the war of 1812. French and American prisoners built the Church of St Michael and All Saints, which was completed in 1815.

Local quarries were exploited to provide granite for all this building work. The stone was also used to build prominent landmarks in London. (Nelson's Column is made of Dartmoor Granite) and Tyrwitt in 1823 opened a horsedrawn tramway to take it down to the docks in Plymouth.

The prison stood empty after the repatriation of the Americans in 1816. The need to house Britain's criminals saw it start receiving convicts in 1850. Many were made to work in the quarries. Conscientious objectors took the place of prisoners released to fight in World War I. Now it is no longer a maximum security prison. Seventy of the 600 inmates are selected to work on the prison farm.

An old toll-house and a Dartmoor pony, Princetown

The old horsedrawn tramway was the basis for a steam railway to Princetown. Opened in 1883, it closed in 1956. The old trackbed makes a good walking route. As you head back to Princetown, aim for the television mast on North Hessary Tor. Erected by the BBC in 1955, it stands 688 foot high.

The Walk

1. Go right to reach the excellent Dartmoor National Park Authority's new High Moorland Visitor Centre (opened by Prince Charles on 9th June, 1993) on your right. Turn right up Plymouth Hill, to pass the Plume of Feathers pub on your left. Cross a cattle grid and pass old toll houses on each side of the road.

2. Bear right, keeping near a fence on your right, to reach the course of the dismantled railway. Turn left along this for one and a half miles.

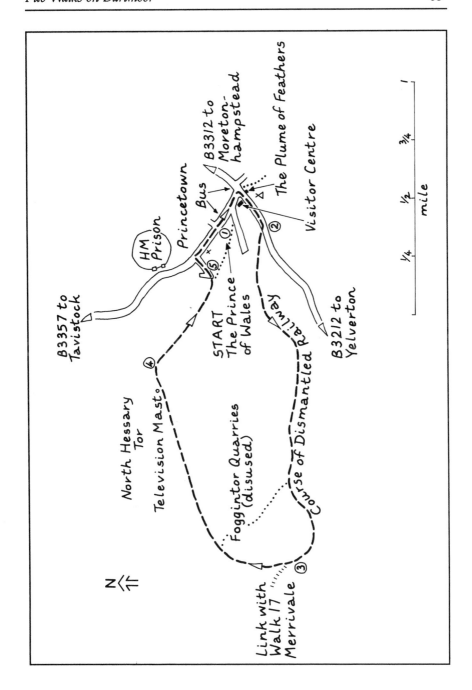

3. Fork right along the firm track to Foggintor Quarry, then turn right across the moor to the television mast on top of North Hessary Tor.

4. Bear right to walk downhill beside a wall on your left. Ignore a stile in it but shortly afterwards do turn left through a kissing-gate which gives access to an estate road.

5. Fork right down the road (Woodville Avenue is the name at its bottom) to the B3357 road near a telephone box. Turn right along the pavement to pass the Church of St Michael and All Saints on your right before reaching the Prince of Wales pub on your right.

19. Wistman's Wood

Route: Two Bridges – Wistman's Wood – Longaford Tor – Two Bridges

Distance: $4^1/2$ miles

Map: O.S. Outdoor Leisure 28 Dartmoor

Start: The Two Bridges Hotel (Grid Reference SX 609750)

Access: Two Bridges is at the junction of the B3212 and the B3357 two miles east of Princetown. Bus no 82 provides a seasonal service from Plymouth and Exeter, on all weekends from late May to mid September, plus Wednesdays in July and early September, then daily during the school summer holidays. Bus no 98 provides a regular weekly service from Tavistock on Fridays throughout the year.

The Two Bridges Hotel (0822 890206)

There has been an inn here for centuries, although the first record is of a Saracen's Head inn in 1805. It used to house a blacksmith's shop. It was developed as a hotel and given its present name in 1893. Real ale, food (including vegetarian dishes) and accommodation are available. The hotel's own real ale is called Prisoner's Poison. Opening hours are 11 am to 3.30 pm and 6 pm to 11 pm on weekdays, noon to 3 pm and 7 pm to 10.30 pm on Sundays.

Wistman's Wood

This is a fascinating area of stunted oaks which, at 1350 foot above sea level, form the last remnants of the ancient forest. As it is a National Nature Reserve, you are asked not to enter it. 'Wistman' is derived from 'wissan', meaning 'to know'. The wisemen, or druids, came here (similarly, Wessex is derived from Gewissae, or Gnostics). Crockern Tor is said to be an ancient meeting place, even when the ancient Greeks came to these parts for tin. It was the assembly point for the Stannary Parliament (the Great Court of the Dartmoor tinners) from 1494 to 1703.

Look out for rabbits, originally brought here by the Normans to provide protein for their tables.

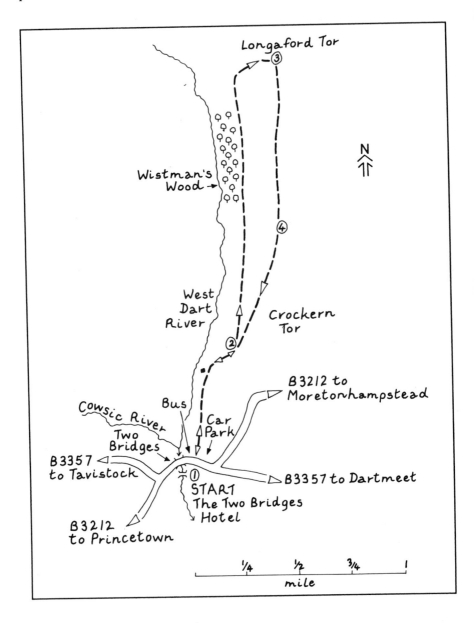

The Walk

1. Cross the road carefully and go through a gate to follow the signposted path up this valley. A firm track leads to a house at Crockern. Bear right to pass the house on your left and follow the signposted path to a wooden step stile.

2. Go ahead over the stile and walk parallel to the river below on your left. Yellow waymarks are painted on rocks. Cross a ladder stile in the wall ahead and reach Wistman's Wood. Pass this on your left before bearing uphill to Longaford Tor.

3. Turn right to walk back along the ridge, passing above Wistman's Wood, now on your right.

4. Cross a ladder stile in a corner formed by two walls ahead. Bear gradually downhill to reach the step stile encountered at direction point 2. Go ahead over it to retrace your steps to the Two Bridges Hotel.

The Two Bridges Hotel

20. Postbridge

Route: Postbridge – Waterfall – Postbridge

Distance: 5 miles

Map: O.S. Outdoor Leisure 28 Dartmoor

Start: The East Dart Hotel (Grid Reference SX 649790)

Access: Postbridge is on the B3212 between Princetown and Moreton-hampstead. There is a seasonal bus service from Plymouth and Exeter. Bus no 82 runs on all weekends from late May to mid September, on Wednesdays in July and mid September and daily during the school summer holidays. Bus no 98 provides a regular weekly service from Tavistock on Fridays throughout the summer.

The East Dart Hotel (0822 88213)

Built as an inn in the early 19th century, this soon became a temperance hotel. Mrs Lizzie Webb, the landlord's wife, was a devoted churchgoer and took to heart a sermon about the demon drink. She persuaded her husband to empty the beer barrels into the East Dart River one night. There was a full moon and legend says a dog appeared on the riverbank, lapped up the beer and gave a great howl. Its ghost is said to reappear at full moon. Alcohol wasn't sold here again until the late 1950s. This is a great place for meeting other walkers. Food, real ale and accommodation are all available. Bar opening hours are 11 am to 11 pm on weekdays, noon to 3 pm and 7 pm to 10.30 pm on Sundays.

Postbridge

A magnificent clapper bridge was built across the river here in the 13th century. The road bridge dates from the end of the 18th century. Drift Lane acquired its name when animals were driven along it before and after periods of grazing on the exposed moorland. The waterfall is a place to refresh yourself on a hot day, when there's nothing to beat a natural shower.

The clapper bridge, Postbridge

The Walk

1. Go left and avoid the road bridge by going left across the Clapper Bridge. Return to the road, cross it carefully and follow the pavement to the car park. Take a stile at the back of this, just to the left of the Dartmoor National Park Information Centre.

2. Turn right along a track which is known as the drift lane. Climb gradually with this for over a mile, having a wall on your left before going through a gate and following a wall on your right. Cross Braddon Lake Stream, keep the wall on your right and bear left, away from it, near the top to reach a stile in the fence ahead (this is to the left of rocks).

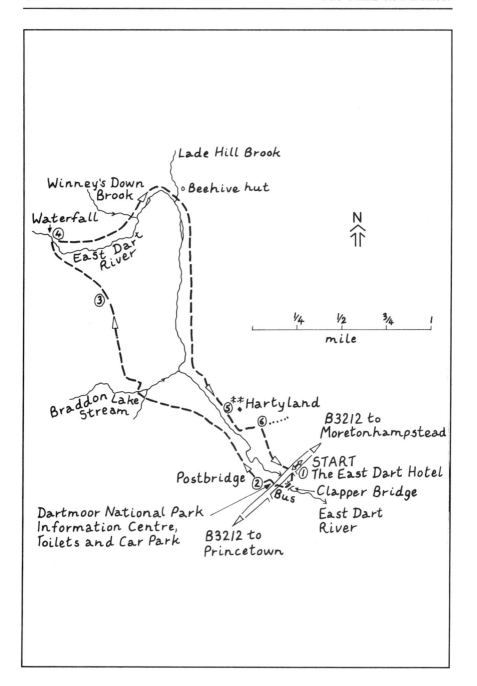

3. Cross the stile and bear slightly left towards a waterfall in the East Dart River. Cross the river above this.

4. A well-trodden path bears right, keeping above the river. Step over Winney's Down Brook, continue through a small gate and follow the river as it bends. Cross another tributary stream (Lade Hill Brook). About 150 yards up this stream (from the confluence), on your right hand side as you face upstream, is a beehive hut. Tinners stored tools and ingots there. Continue downstream above the East Dart River on your right.

5. Take a gate to follow a short path past a plantation of conifer trees on your left. Emerge through a second gate and continue with the river on your right. Take a gate ahead and turn left, as signposted.

6. Turn right at another signpost in the corner of this field. Go ahead through a gate and reach the B3212 road. Turn left along it to return to the East Dart Hotel.

21. Widecombe in the Moor

Route: Widecombe in the Moor – Hameldon Beacon – Grimspound -Natsworthy Manor – Widecombe in the Moor

Distance: $7^1/_2$ miles

Map: O.S. Outdoor Leisure 28 Dartmoor

Start: The Old Inn (Grid Reference SX 717767)

Access: Widecombe in the Moor is at the end of the B3387 road six miles west of Bovey Tracey, from where there are buses (no 171 on summer Sundays and no 193 from Mondays to Fridays).

The Old Inn (0364 2207)

Widecombe Wallop is just one of the real ales on offer here. Food is also available and the opening hours are 11 am to 3 pm and 6 pm to 11 pm on weekdays, noon to 3 pm and 7 pm to 10.30 pm on Sundays. Known to date from at least the 14th century, the present building was rebuilt after a fire in 1977. It has retained its atmosphere but not the ghost of Harry, who was murdered here. He was often seen in the kitchen before the fire. Listen and you may hear the sobs of a girl from an upstairs bedroom. She may be Kitty Day, a girl who hanged herself after being made pregnant by a local land owner's son in the 18th century.

Widecombe in the Moor

Few places are as famous as Widecombe, yet so tiny. The Fair is still held on the second Tuesday of each September. it inspired the song that is known all over the English-speaking world and whose tune most readily enters the mind as one tramps these moors. Here are the words:

Widecombe Fair

Tom Pearce, Tom Pearce, lend me your grey mare,
All along, down along, out along lee.
For I want to go to Widecombe Fair,
Wi'Bill Brewer, Jan Stewer, Peter Gurney,
Peter Davy, Dan'l Whiddon, Harry Hawk,
Old Uncle Tom Cobley and all,
Old Uncle Tom Cobley and all.

And when shall I see again my grey mare?
All along, down along, out along lee.
By Friday soon or Saturday noon,
Wi'Bill brewer, Jan Stewer, etc.

Then Friday came and Saturday noon,
All along, down along, out along lee.
Tom Pearce's old mare hath not trotted home
Wi'Bill Brewer, Jan Stewer, etc.

So Tom Pearce he got up to the top of the hill,
All along, down along, out along lee.
And he see's his old mare a-making her will
Wi'Bill Brewer, Jan Stewer, etc.

So Tom Pearce's old mare, her took sick and died,
All along, out along, down along lee.
And Tom he sat down on a stone and he cried,
Wi'Bill Brewer, Jan Stewer, etc.

But this isn't the end of this shocking affair,
All along, down along, out along lee.
Nor, though they be dead, of the horrid career -
of Bill Brewer, Jan Stewer, etc.

When the wind whistles cold on the moor of a night,
All along, down along, out along lee.
Tom Pearce's old mare doth appear gashly white -
Wi'Bill Brewer, Jan Stewer, etc.

And all the long night be heard skirling and groans,
All along, down along, out along lee.
From Tom pearce's old mare in her rattling bones,
And from Bill Brewer, Jan Stewer, etc.

The Church of St Pancras fits the bill with its mighty tower earning it the sobriquet 'Cathedral of the Moors'. Dartmoor ponies may be seen grazing in its shadow. Prehistoric men knew the surrounding downs and buried their dead at Broad Barrow, on the 1745 foot summit of Hamel Down. Cattle were kept in a compound during the winter at Grimspound in the Bronze Age. Twenty-four circular houses also stood here. Their low stone walls remain but the conical roofs, probably made of thatch, bracken or heather, supported by a central pole, have disappeared. As well as grazing cattle the pound's Bronze Age inhabitants may have been in the tin trade. The climate was kinder then, while the lower land was under forest. Nevertheless, it is remarkable to find such a settlement at 1530 foot above sea level.

Approaching the Old Inn, Widdecombe

The Walk

1. Go left and turn left on the lane to Natsworthy. After 200 yards, turn left on the lane signposted as the path to Hameldown for Grimspound.

2. Go ahead through a gate to follow the path over the moor, keeping a wall on your right.

3. When the wall bears right, go ahead along a broad, grassy, track, ignoring a cross path.

4. Ignore the lane and bear right to walk uphill to reach Hameldon beacon (1697 foot above sea level).

5. Bear left along the ridgeway and pass Broad Barrow on the way to Hameldown Tor. This is part of the Two Moors Way (a long distance path of some 102 miles between Ivybridge, Dartmoor, and Lynmouth, Exmoor).

6. Descend to the circular enclosure of Grimspound.

7. Turn right along a sandy track and continue past a memorial stone to the crew of an RAF bomber that crashed here on the way home from France on 22nd March, 1941.

8. Bear right along a road, passing Natsworthy Manor on your right. This road leads back to Widecombe.

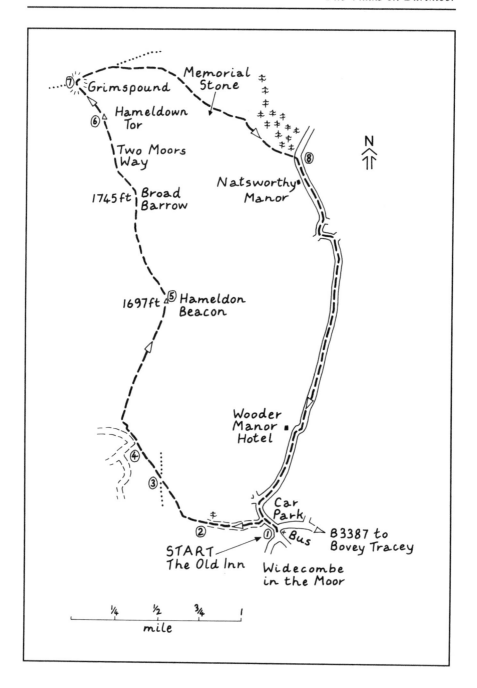

Grimspound

Memorial Stone

⑦

⑥ Hameldown Tor

Two Moors Way

1745 ft   Broad Barrow

Natsworthy Manor

⑧

1697ft ⑤ Hameldon Beacon

N ↑

Wooder Manor Hotel

④

③

②

Car Park

START The Old Inn

① Bus

B 3387 to Bovey Tracey

Widecombe in the Moor

¼   ½   ¾   1

mile

22. Haytor

Route: The Rock Inn, Haytor Vale – Haytor Rocks – Dismantled Tramway – The Rock Inn, Haytor Vale

Distance: 3 miles

Map: O.S. Outdoor Leisure 28 Dartmoor

Start: The Rock Inn, Haytor Vale (Grid Reference SX 771772)

Access: Haytor Vale is just below the B3387 about three miles west of Bovey Tracey. There is a turning near the Moorland Hotel, as well as a car park beside the B3387 just to the west of this hotel. Buses stop at the Moorland Hotel (although some also stop at the Rock Inn down in the vale). No 171 runs between Newton Abbot and Widecombe on summer Sundays, while no 193 links Newton Abbot and Widecombe via Haytor's Moorland Hotel from Mondays to Fridays, with some buses calling at the Rock Inn, Haytor Vale, on Wednesdays and Fridays.

The Rock Inn, Haytor Vale (0364 661305)

This early 19th century coaching inn is a great favourite with ramblers. Muddy boots are best left in the foyer, however. This is the place to choose for overnight accommodation if you are interested in ghosts. Mrs Thatcher and her entourage stayed here a few years ago and it made an appearance for one of her Special Branch detectives. He didn't know of the ghost, thought it was a real person and shot it. The result was a hole in the ceiling. The poor ghost is that of Belinda, a serving wench here in the 19th century. She had an affair with a coachman who was, unfortunately, already married. His wife discovered them and beat Belinda to death on the stairs. The original purpose of the inn was to provide relaxation for the workers in Templer's quarry, Haytor. You can enjoy real ale and food here, including the pub's very own Rock Bitter, between 11 am and 2.30 pm, then 6.30 pm to 11 pm on weekdays, noon to 3 pm and 7 pm to 10.30 pm on Sundays.

The Moorland Hotel, Haytor (0364 661407)

This is another place offering overnight accommodation, but without a ghost. Food and real ale are available. Bar opening times are 11 am to 2.30 pm and 6 pm to 11 pm on weekdays, noon to 3 pm and 7 pm to 10.30 pm on Sundays. Agatha Christie completed her first detective novel, *The Mysterious Affair at Styles*, here and a lounge with a stylish cocktail bar is named after her. The hotel reopened in 1984 after a fire in 1970.

Haytor Rocks

Haytor

Stone from the quarries around Haytor can now be seen in some of the most famous buildings in London, such as the British Museum and the National Gallery. There is now a long distance walking route, known as the Templer Way, tracing the route taken by the granite from the quarries to the port at Shaldon, across the mouth of the estuary from

Teignmouth. The canal and tramway forming this route were built by the Templer family, local landowners. The Stover Canal was originally dug, between 1790 and 1792, to serve the local clay industry. As granite found a market in the imposing buildings of the rapidly growing cities, a tramway was built to bring it from Haytor down to the canal in 1820. The canal gave access to the ports in the Teign estuary. The quarries and tramway fell into disuse by 1858 because of cheaper competition from Cornwall. You can still see the old tramway, whose 'rails' are made of granite. There is even a junction, where an iron blade was inserted in a hole in the granite rail to act as a primitive form of 'points'. The granite was shaped to guide the wheels of the horse-drawn wagons. The wheels were flat and the 'rails' were flanged (the opposite to modern railway practice). The old London Bridge that is now in America is built of Haytor granite.

'Ponts' in the old granite tramway, Haytor

The Walk

1. Go right to follow the lane up to a T-junction opposite the Moorland Hotel. Turn right over a cattle grid to reach the B3387 and go left along it, passing a telephone box and the bus stop on your left. Reach a car park on your left.

2. Bear right, away from the road, on a well-trodden path to Haytor Rocks. Continue to reach the course of the old tramway.

3. Turn right to follow the tramway. Look out for the junction with the line coming from your left. Reach another junction where a line comes in from your right. Go ahead down to a road.

4. Bear right to the Moorland Hotel's road junction and turn left here to retrace your steps to the Rock Inn down in the vale.

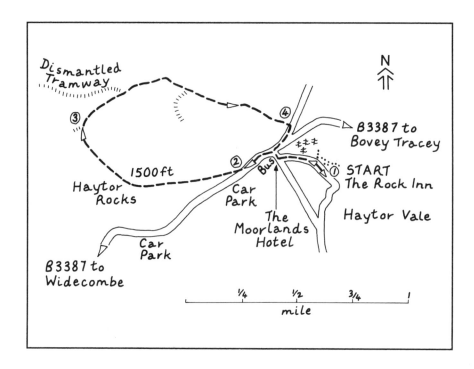

23. Horrabridge

Route: Horrabridge – Monkswell – Huckworthy Common – Knowle Down -Horrabridge

Distance: 5 miles

Maps: O.S. Outdoor Leisure 28 Dartmoor

Start: The Leaping Salmon (Grid Reference SX 513700)

Access: Horrabridge is beside the A386 between Tavistock and Plymouth, along which there is an excellent daily bus service (nos 83, 84, and 84A). Some buses go into the village to stop near The Leaping Salmon.

The Leaping Salmon (0822 852939)

This pub used to be known locally as 'The Starving Pig'. The landlord in 1945 kept pigs but didn't feed them much. One pig used to escape regularly and beg for food in the bar. The pub's real name then was The New Inn (new in 1746). It changed its name in 1951. There are some fish kept in tanks in the lounge. There's a kiddies cabin in the beer garden, while food and real ale are both available. Opening hours are 11 am to 11 pm on weekdays, noon to 3 pm and 7 pm to 10.30 pm on Sundays.

Horrabridge

There really are salmon in the River Walkham. Horrabridge is traditionally a busy little place, frequented by miners, including an early example of a shaft mine which operated on Furze Hill in the 16th century. The local oakwoods were also coppiced to produce large quantities of charcoal and tanning bark for a local tanyard. The river was a source of water power.

The Leaping Salmon, Horrabridge

The Walk

1. Go left to pass the bridge over the River Walkham on your right. Fork left up Jordan Lane and come to a farm track on your left.

2. Bear right along the waymarked footpath to Sampford Spiney. This old green lane passes a large house called Monkswell. Continue through a farmyard to follow a track to a road.

3. Go ahead across the road and up stone steps to take a waymarked stile. Descend into a farmyard and take the enclosed path which leads along the top of a steep meadow before being down to a stream. Keep this stream on your right as you continue to another road.

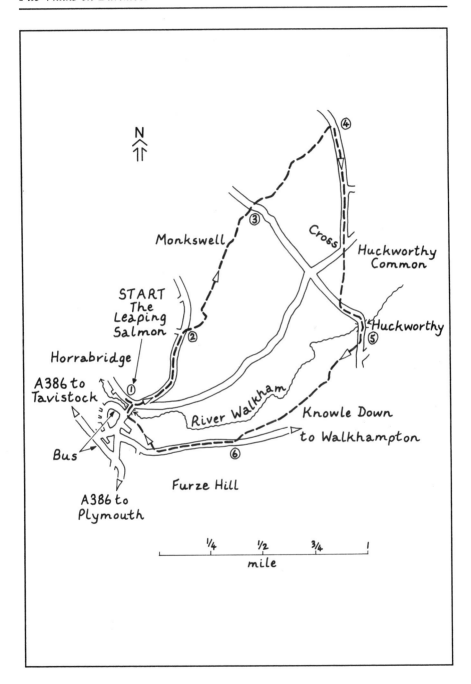

4. Go right along the road, ignore a turning on your left and reach a cross by a cattle grid, at the next junction. Leave the road here by going straight ahead across Huckworthy Common. Go down a stony track to a road which leads to Huckworthy Bridge.

5. Follow the road for 200 yards beyond the bridge, then turn right along the signposted track for Horrabridge. Take stepping-stones over a stream and bear left uphill to continue with an enclosed track. Emerge from the bracken of Knowle Down onto the road between Horrabridge and Walkhampton at a cattle grid.

6. Bear right along the road for Horrabridge and take a footpath on your right to pass playing-fields and reach the River Walkham near the bridge which you cross to return to the Leaping Salmon.

24. Meavy

Route: Meavy – Burrator Reservoir – Sheepston – Marchant's Cross -Meavy

Distance: 4 miles

Maps: O.S. Outdoor Leisure 28 Dartmoor

Start: The Royal Inn (Grid Reference SX 541672)

Access: Meavy is two miles by very minor road to the east of the A386 at Yelverton, from where there is a good bus service (no 56) on weekdays.

The Royal Oak (0822 852944)

This is one of the few pubs in Britain to be owned by a parish council. It may have been built as long ago as 1122 when the nearby church of St Peter was constructed. The present building is redolent of the Tudors and there is a record of ale and wine sold here in 1589 to a workman on Drake's Leat. This stone water-channel was built to supply Plymouth with water. Burrator Reservoir dates from 1898 (and was enlarged in 1928). Before the Dissolution, monks and pilgrims would have found hospitality here on their way between the abbeys of Buckfast and Tavistock.

The nearby oak tree, from which the inn is named, accompanied an old preaching stone by the green and is said to date from the reign of King John. Its hollow trunk was used around 1900 to store peat. Some say that an old wood shed at one end of the pub was where lepers were fed through a special feeding slot. You can feed here in more comfortable conditions today, while real ale is served. Opening hours are 11 am to 2.30 pm and 6 pm to 11 pm on weekdays, noon to 3 pm and 7 pm to 10.30 pm on Sundays.

The Royal Oak, Meavy

The 'White Rajahs'

This area is where the first two 'White Rajahs' of Sarawak, Sir Jones and Sir Charles Brooke came to their final rest. Their imposing tombs are in the churchyard of St Leonard's, Sheepstor. The Brooke family ruled Sarawak, in Northern Borneo, as hereditary rajahs from 1841 to 1945.

Marchant's Cave

Pilgrims fortified themselves with prayers at this cross before setting foot on the wilds of Dartmoor. Eight feet high and with two crosses carved on each face, it was called the Smalacumbacrosse in 1291.

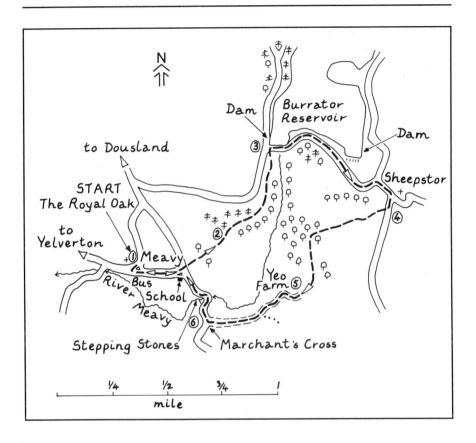

The Walk

1. Go right and pay your respects to the old oak tree before turning left along the road which passes the school on your right just before a junction. Bear slightly left to go ahead along a footpath whose start is hidden by a hedge, (there is a gate, but not on the right of way). Cross a meadow.

2. Follow the path waymarked in yellow through the trees. This bears left on a twisting route to the dried bed of the leat that supplied Plymouth with its water in the 16th century. Continue with this, then climb above it to reach the road near the dam of Burrator Reservoir.

3. Turn right to walk with the reservoir on your left. Bear right at a fork to reach the village of Sheepstor. Turn right along Portland Lane, going south and soon crossing a stream.

4. Turn right along the signposted public footpath to Marchant's Cross. After a short stretch of lane, bear left to cross a field diagonally to a gate, as waymarked. Continue over steps in a wall to follow orange waymarks through woodland. Emerge over another wall and down an enclosed path. Take a stile on your left to skirt a field and descend to Yeo Farm.

5. Follow the farm's access lane to reach the road at Marchant's Cross.

6. Go right to follow the road back to the T-junction where you turn left for Meavy. If dry, take the short cut across the River Meavy by going over the stepping-stones.

25. Buckfast Abbey

Route: Buckfastleigh – Bilberry Hill Copse – St Mary's Abbey, Buckfast – Buckfastleigh

Distance: 4¹/₂ miles

Maps: O.S. Outdoor Leisure 28 Dartmoor, O.S. Pathfinder 1341, Buckfastleigh

Start: The Waterman's Arms, Buckfastleigh (Grid Reference SX 736662)

Access: Buckfastleigh is just off the A38, between Exeter and Plymouth and near its junction with the A384 from Totnes. You could come by steam train during the summer from Totnes on the Dart Valley Light Railway (tel 0803 555872). Bus no X39 runs to Buckfastleigh from Exeter and Plymouth on a daily basis.

The Waterman's Arms (0364 43200)

This congenial pub is haunted by a woman who frequents a corner of the Dartmoor Lounge, as well as patronising the betting shop next door. Real ale, food and bed and breakfast are available. Opening hours are 11 am to 3 pm and 5 pm to 11 pm on weekdays, noon to 3 pm and 7 pm to 10.30 pm on Sundays.

Buckfast Abbey

This is a living monastery, revived since monks returned here in 1882. The first recorded monastery was founded in 1018, when Cnut was on the throne. The abbey was transferred to the Cistercians in 1147 and the present buildings are modelled on theirs, which fell into ruin at the Dissolution in 1539. There is a free audio visual presentation near the bookshop plus an exhibition (small fee) in the church crypt. The monks live by the labour of their own hands and the abbey is well known for its stained glass windows (made here for many other places), honey and tonic wine.

Buckfast Abbey

The Walk

1. Go ahead from the crossroads to follow Jordan Street (signposted for Hapstead), passing Market Street (signposted for Holne) on your right. Pass Royal Oak Guest House on your left. Continue along what has become a country lane to pass a house called Merryfield on your right. Ignore the lane for Wootton on your left but immediately after it bear right through a kissing-gate beside a fieldgate. Take the signposted public footpath across the narrow field.

2. Go through the gate into woodland and follow the path which soon bears left and climbs to a path junction. Fork left downhill, emerge over a stile and continue, as signposted, across a footbridge and another narrow field to take a kissing-gate to reach the lane.

3. Turn right along the lane and immediately ignore a left fork signposted for Camphill Devon Community. Your lane is for Bilberry Hill. The metalled surface peters out when you reach a house on your right. Go ahead through a gate to follow a track. Maintain your direction, as signposted, by walking with a hedge on your left and past fields on your right.

4. Continue through Bilberry Hill Copse. Emerge over a stile and walk with a hedge on your right, then bear right through the gates of Button Farm. Go through its yard and down its drive to a lane.

5. Turn right along the lane to descend past Brook Mill on your left. Climb to the crossroads at Hockmoor Head and cross the Holne -Buckfast road to take a lane ahead. This goes downhill to another road junction, where you bear right.

6. Reach the crossroads at Fritz's Grave (was Fritz a monk who committed suicide? Suicides were buried where leys crossed, in order to dissipate the negative energies). Turn left for Buckfast and go all the way down to the abbey. Go right into its grounds through the North Gate. Pass the Abbey Church on your left and leave through the South Gate.

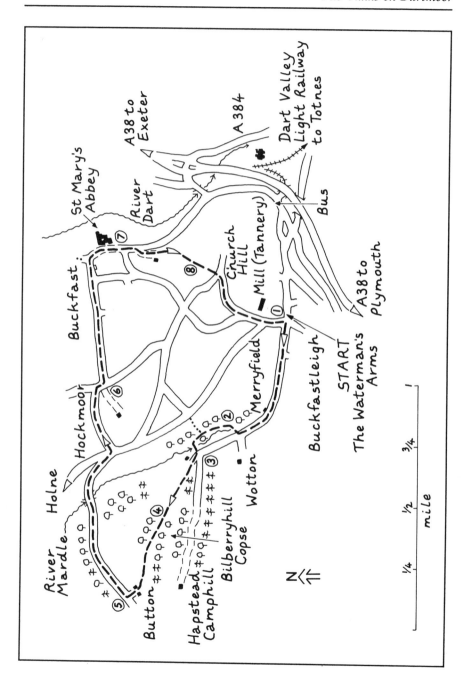

7. Bear left to pass the Post Office on your left then, immediately after the Mill Carpet Shop on your left, bear right across the road and up the signposted path to Church Hill. After passing houses on your right this becomes a narrow footpath with kissing-gates.

8. Emerge in the corner of a field and go ahead along its top ridge beside a hedge on your right. Reach a road and go left 10 yards to a junction. Turn sharply right down Church Hill back into Buckfastleigh. Go ahead past a tanning mill on your left to return to the corner at which the Waterman's Arms is on your left.

26. South Brent

Route: South Brent – Lydia Bridge – Shipley Bridge – Didworthy – Lutton – South Brent

Distance: 5 miles

Map: O.S. Outdoor Leisure 28 Dartmoor

Start: The Anchor Inn (Grid Reference SX 698602)

Access: South Brent is on the B3372 which feeds into the A38 between Exeter and Plymouth. There is a good weekday bus service (no X80) from Plymouth and Torquay.

The Anchor Inn (0364 73135)

Navy gangs 'pressed' men into service here in the 19th century hence the name. There are rumours of tunnels running from under the pub, so that regulars could escape, or hide until the coast was clear.

The Anchor Inn

Badly damaged by fire in 1990, the inn has been well restored and has retained its character. Real ale and food are served. Opening hours are 11 am to 3.30 pm and 6 pm to 11 pm from Mondays to Thursdays, 11 am to 11 pm on Fridays and Saturdays, noon to 3 pm and 7 pm to 10.30 pm.

South Brent

This old market town with its fine Norman church on the southern edge of Dartmoor has been a channel for drovers, probably for thousands of years until relatively recently. People probably lived in the South Hams area during the winter and drove their herds and flocks up into Dartmoor for summer grazing. The importance of this access to the central plateaux may be highlighted by the system of reaves, as outlined in the Introduction.

The Walk

1. Go right, along Church Street. Take the signposted public footpath to Lydia Bridge that bears left under the railway bridge. Take a kissing-gate to walk under the trees beside the River Avon, on your left, upstream to Lydia Bridge. Join the road to go left across the bridge.

2. Bear right at a fork and follow this road up the valley, above the river on your right. Ignore two turnings on your left and a bridge giving access to Didworthy across the river. Follow the road as it bears right to cross Shipley Bridge.

3. Turn right to follow the signposted public footpath to Lutton via Didworthy. Take a gate and continue over a stile. Bear slightly left to climb another stile and go ahead through woodland. Cross two more stiles and go through a gate.

4. Cross a lane to follow a track ahead to Didworthy. Bear right to pass a house on your left. Continue along a lane which changes to a track as it climbs. Walk above Overbrent Wood on an enclosed path. Go ahead through gates and down to a ford, then up a track into Lutton.

5. Go right at a junction with a road to follow it down the valley back to South Brent and the Anchor Inn.

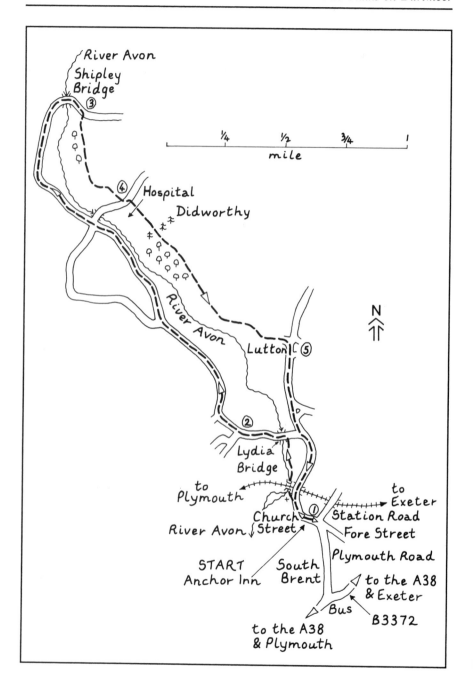

27. Ivybridge

Route: Ivybridge – Harford – Hangershell Rock – Two Moors Way -Ivybridge

Distance: $6^1/_2$ miles

Maps: O.S. Pathfinder 1357 Ivybridge, O.S. Outdoor Leisure 28 Dartmoor

Start: The Exchange (Grid Reference SX 635562)

Access: Ivybridge is on the B3213 which feeds into the A38 between Plymouth and Exeter. There is a good weekday bus service (no X80) from Plymouth and Torquay.

The Exchange (0752 896677)

Bed and breakfast accommodation is available in this pub which also provides food and real ale. Take note of the opening days and hours. This pub is only open in the evening (7 pm to 11 pm) from Monday to Thursday inclusive. It is open from noon to 3 pm and from 7 pm to 11 pm on Fridays, between noon and 11 pm on Saturdays and at the usual times on a Sunday (noon to 3 pm and 7 pm to 10.30 pm).

The Bridge Inn (0752 897086)

This very friendly pub is open for real ale and other drinks on every weekday between 11 am and 11 pm (noon to 3 pm and 7 pm to 10.30 pm on Sundays). There is a beer garden and pub games (pool, darts) are played, but food and accommodation are not available. The inn used to be the old village bakery.

Ivybridge

This town grew around the papermill in the 19th century. Now it is the southern terminus of the Two Moors Way. This long distance path of some 102 miles crosses Dartmoor and Exeter to reach Lynmouth. The old tramway it follows just north of Ivybridge was constructed in 1910 to serve the Redlake china clay works. It was closed in 1932.

The Walk

1. Go right to cross the bridge over the River Erme. Turn left (leaving The Bridge Inn on the B3213 on your right) to walk upstream with the river on your left. Follow the Two Moors Way along the steeply rising road to Harford, passing the paper mill on your left and the school on your right. Cross the railway.

2. Do not turn right with the Two Moors Way. You will return along it. Meanwhile, go ahead along the road to Harford, where there is a beautiful church dedicated to the Celtic St Petroc.

3. Turn right to pass the church on your left. Go up this lane to the car park at Harford Moor Gate. Faced with featureless and pathless moorland, stand square with the lane behind you and aim for the prominent tor of Hangershell Rock ahead. Skirt around to the left of a boggy area below the tor. Reach the firm trackbed of an old tramway.

4. Turn right to follow this old tramway (part of the Two Moors Way) for one mile. Go round a long curve, initially to the right, then bearing left. Look out for when it bears right again, where a small section of stone wall on your right and boulders on your left indicate an ancient enclosure and hut circles. Fork right here to leave the old tramway but stay with the Two Moors Way. Descend to a gate.

5. Go down the walled track to join the road from Harford to Ivybridge and retrace your steps into the town. Pass the Bridge Inn on your left before bearing right across the bridge to The Exchange.

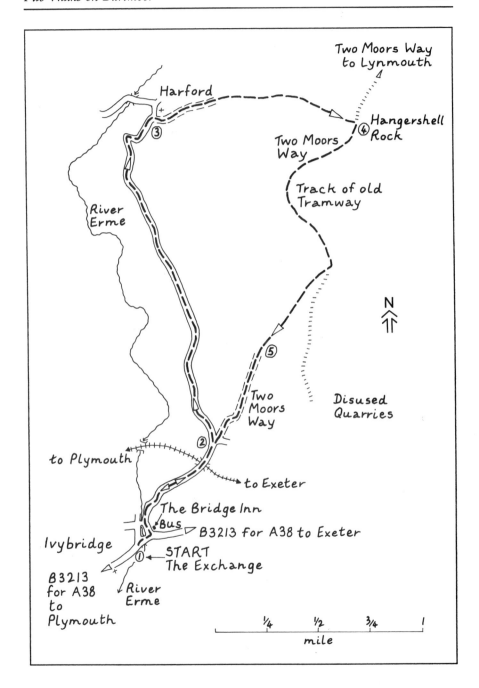

The Exchange

We publish a wide range of titles, including general interest publications, guides to individual towns, and books for outdoor activities centred on walking and cycling in the great outdoors throughout England and Wales. This is a recent selection:

General interest:

THE INCREDIBLY BIASED BEER GUIDE – Ruth Herman
This is the most comprehensive guide to Britain's smaller breweries and the pubs where you can sample their products. Produced with the collaboration of the Small Independent Brewers' Association and including a half-price subscription to The Beer Lovers' Club. *£6.95*

DIAL 999 – EMERGENCY SERVICES IN ACTION – John Creighton
Re-live the excitement as fire engines rush to disasters. See dramatic rescues on land and sea. Read how the professionals keep a clear head and swing into action. *£9.95*

THE ALABAMA AFFAIR – David Hollett
This is an account of Britain's rôle in the American Civil War. Read how Merseyside dockyards supplied ships for the Confederate navy, thereby supporting the slave trade. The *Alabama* was the most famous of the 'Laird Rams', and was chased half-way across the world before being sunk ignominiously. *£9.95*

PEAK DISTRICT DIARY – Roger Redfern
An evocative book, celebrating the glorious countryside of the Peak District. The book is based on Roger's popular column in *The Guardian* newspaper and is profusely illustrated with stunning photographs. *£6.95*

I REMAIN, YOUR SON JACK – J. C. Morten (edited by Sheila Morten)
A collection of almost 200 letters, as featured on BBC TV, telling the moving story of a young soldier in the First World War. Profusely illustrated with contemporary photographs. *£8.95*

FORGOTTEN DIVISIONS – John Fox
A unique account of the 1914 – 18 War, drawing on the experience of soldiers and civilians, from a Lancashire town and a Rhineland village. The book is well illustrated and contains many unique photographs. *£9.95*

ROAD SENSE – Doug Holland
A book for drivers with some experience, preparing them for an advanced driving test. The book introduces a recommended system of car control, based on that developed by the Police Driving School. Doug Holland is a highly qualified driving instructor, working with RoSPA. *£5.95*

Books of Walks:

RAMBLES IN NORTH WALES
– Roger Redfern

HERITAGE WALKS IN THE PEAK DISTRICT
– Clive Price

EAST CHESHIRE WALKS
– Graham Beech

WEST CHESHIRE WALKS
– Jen Darling

WEST PENNINE WALKS
– Mike Cresswell

STAFFORDSHIRE WALKS
– Les Lumsdon

NEWARK AND SHERWOOD RAMBLES
– Malcolm McKenzie

NORTH NOTTINGHAMSHIRE RAMBLES
– MAlcolm McKenzie

RAMBLES AROUND NOTTINGHAM & DERBY
– Keith Taylor

RAMBLES AROUND MANCHESTER
– Mike Cresswell

WESTERN LAKELAND RAMBLES
– Gordon Brown

WELSH WALKS:
Dolgellau and the Cambrian Coast
– Laurence Main and Morag Perrott *(£5.95)*

WELSH WALKS:
Aberystwyth and District
– Laurence Main and Morag Perrott *(£5.95)*

MOSTLY DOWNHILL:
Leisurely walks in the Lake District
– Alan Pears

WEST PENNINE WALKS
– Mike Cresswell

CHALLENGING WALKS IN NORTH-WEST BRITAIN
– Ron Astley *(£9.95)*

WALKING PEAKLAND TRACKWAYS
– Mike Cresswell *(£7.95)*

– all of the above books are currently £6.95 each (except where noted)

LONG-DISTANCE WALKS:

THE GREATER MANCHESTER BOUNDARY WALK
– Graham Phythian

THE THIRLMERE WAY
– Tim Cappelli

THE FURNESS TRAIL
– Tim Cappelli

THE MARCHES WAY
– Les Lumsdon

THE TWO ROSES WAY
– Peter Billington, Eric Slater, Bill Greenwood and Clive Edwards

THE RED ROSE WALK
– Tom Schofield

FROM WHARFEDALE TO WESTMORLAND:
Historical walks through the Yorkshire Dales
– Aline Watson

THE WEST YORKSHIRE WAY
– Nicholas Parrott

– all £6.95 each